D1366419

Aspects of
Sino-American Relations
Since 1784

Also by Thomas H. Etzold

THE CONDUCT OF AMERICAN FOREIGN RELATIONS:
THE OTHER SIDE OF DIPLOMACY

CHINA IN THE 1920S: NATIONALISM AND REVOLUTION
(edited with F. Gilbert Chan)

ASPECTS OF
SINO-AMERICAN
RELATIONS
SINCE 1784

Edited by Thomas H. Etzold

New Viewpoints
A Division of Franklin Watts
New York / London / 1978

New Viewpoints
A Division of Franklin Watts
730 Fifth Avenue
New York, New York 10019

Library of Congress Cataloging in Publication Data

Main entry under title:

Aspects of Sino-American relations since 1784.

  Includes bibliographies and index.
  1. United States—Foreign relations—China—Ad-
dresses, essays, lectures. 2. China—Foreign rela-
tions—United States—Addresses, essays, lectures. 3.
Chinese Americans—History—Addresses, essays, lec-
tures.
I. Etzold, Thomas H.
E183.8.C5A79   327.51'073   77–15586
ISBN 0–531–05399–7
ISBN 0–531–05609–0 pbk.

Copyright © 1978 by Thomas H. Etzold
All rights reserved
Printed in the United States of America
5 4 3 2 1

DEC 1 3 1979

For Suzanne, Klaus, and Ingrid

Preface

In recent years the Sino-American relationship has commanded increasing attention both within and without government, and rightfully so. It is apparent that China has reached a new level of influence in regional affairs. In attaining enhanced regional power, China has also exerted increased influence beyond East Asia, for a stronger China has affected substantially the interests and mutual relations of the Soviet Union, the United States, and Japan.

Because the Sino-American relationship has been growing in importance both to China's leaders and to America's, it is particularly necessary to understand the legacy that burdens, and to a certain extent constrains, that relation. It is a cause for concern, though certainly not for despair, that the principal feature of that legacy insofar as it derives from American policy is ambiguous; for American intentions in Asia in general, and toward China in particular, have been hazy, and policies and actions inconsistent.

The haziness of American policy in the Far East, and its confusing legacy, indeed form the theme of the six essays presented here. In Chapter One, William J. Brinker discusses aspects of interaction between Asian trade and cultural cross-fertilization, and points to the meager understanding of Asian culture resulting from the first one hundred years of American contact. In Chapter Two, Frederick B. Hoyt and Eugene P. Trani highlight the doubly confusing issue of Chinese immigration to the United States: Chinese immigrants were uncertain of their reception, and Americans were ambivalent about the combination of liabilities and advantages evident in the influx of Chinese. The open door, one of the most enduring and least ambiguous-seeming tenets of American policy in the Far East, appears somewhat less than clear and consistent in Chapter Three by Raymond A. Esthus.

In Chapters Four and Five, David F. Trask and the present author demonstrate how circumstances, unpredictable and uncontrollable, have distorted the orderly plans and expectations of American political and military leaders, in this way giving an impression of inconsistency in American policy in Paris in 1918–1919 and in American strategy for the Far East in 1948–1951.

Finally, in Chapter Six, Jerome K. Holloway, Jr. and the present writer survey the long course of America's relations with the Communist leaders of China, arguing that fluctuations on the surface of these relations have obscured the structural continuities of the association, with the result that Americans of the present day may possess confused and unrealistic expectations for the future of Sino-American relations.

In discussing the uncertain aspects of the long Sino-American relationship, the authors of these essays have emphasized interpretation and striven for brevity, at least by academic standards. The essays do not pretend to be conclusive. They will, one hopes, help lift the haze surrounding America's relations with China.

T.H.E.

Acknowledgments

The editor acknowledges with thanks several obligations incurred in preparing this volume of essays. Will Davison, executive editor at New Viewpoints, from the outset was interested in the proposal for the project and, together with his reader, made valuable suggestions for improving the essays here presented. John Lewis Gaddis of the Naval War College and Ohio University (Athens) commented on Chapter Five. Mary Prasso, Diane Cote, Agnes Gilman, and Deanna May helped prepare portions of the typescript. Jerome K. Holloway, Jr., a contributor to this volume, was a regular, reliable source of advice and information. Suzanne Burdick Etzold listened a lot, read and proofread copy and galleys, eliminated errors, and suggested improvements, especially to Chapters Five and Six.

T.H.E.

Contents

Aspects of
Sino-American Relations
Since 1784

Chapter One

Commerce, Culture, and Horticulture: The Beginnings of Sino-American Cultural Relations

BY WILLIAM J. BRINKER

In addition to financial wealth and commercial success, the China trade of the eighteenth and nineteenth centuries brought to Americans the beginnings of direct cultural associations. These associations were often modish, tentative, and superficial in their impact on the American public. Confusion about the significance of Chinese history, uncertainty over the aims of the Chinese government, and an inability to comprehend Asian literature and art were characteristic among Americans of the nineteenth century. To an extent these characteristics have prevailed into the twentieth century, as current fads of fashion, sport, religion, and medicine demonstrate. Experts declare that Americans as well as other Westerners do not understand the Asian setting from which these activities or ideas emerged and therefore can neither comprehend nor experience them fully. Acupuncture, kung fu, and Zen may not have guided Secretary of State Henry Kissinger to China, but Ping-Pong players did become unofficial emissaries in an unusual example of "cultural diplomacy." In all of this, the beginnings of Asian influence on culture in the United States have received scant attention, and even less understanding.

Asian influences on American life require cautious study, for until the twentieth century, what Americans believed to be

3

Oriental culture was rarely authentic. Americans inherited distorted ideas about the Orient from their European forebears, especially the British, and later, direct contact through trade did little to alter them. During the early years of United States-Chinese trade, Americans eagerly sought goods superior in quality to those produced in the United States and Europe as well as goods unobtainable outside of East Asia. But Chinese goods intended for export manifested different—even indifferent—standards of taste and quality. When, occasionally, quality goods suited to Chinese taste did reach the United States, they all too often remained unrecognized and unappreciated amidst inferior and sometimes fraudulent items. Similarly, Oriental ideas and practices remained inaccessible to American comprehension. Until the end of the nineteenth century, the United States lacked the institutions necessary to accumulate, interpret, digest, and absorb things Chinese or Japanese. The understanding or sympathy that did occur was due to some few extraordinary individuals. The result was accidental, perhaps haphazard. Throughout the nineteenth century this limited and uncertain cultural contact had little influence on early Sino-American relations.

European perceptions and contacts helped to distort colonial America's view of East Asia. From the time of Marco Polo's travels to the end of the eighteenth century, written accounts by Europeans of travels in the Orient produced two visions of far Cathay: It was a land of exotic flora and fauna and wealthy beyond belief; or, alternatively, it was a land of harmony, stability, and reason. By the sixteenth century the Portuguese had established trading contacts in southern China. European Jesuit missionaries followed quickly. In their enthusiasm for China and its institutions, the missionaries became propagandists and transmitted to the West an uncritical view of Oriental culture.

In the eighteenth century, interest in things Chinese ran high, especially in France. In 1700 a "Chinese Fête" held at Versailles ushered in the "Chinese century." In the hands of Voltaire, Confucius became an archetype of the eighteenth-century rationalist. François Quesnay and his followers, the physiocrats, became students of Chinese culture. This study led Quesnay to publish *Le Despotisme de la Chine* in which he proposed economic and political reforms to strengthen the French monarchy. Benevolent despotism in the Chinese manner seemed the answer. This Sinomania was bound to encourage reaction. Toward the end of the eighteenth century, British views challenged prevailing attitudes toward China. Early British encounters with Chinese officials contradicted the Jesuit-inspired image. In place of fantasy or eulogy, British mercantile and diplomatic accounts stressed misgovernment, corruption, and degeneracy in a nation that imperiously brushed aside British attempts to establish trade and diplomatic relations in the European mode. Thus, depending on his source of impressions, the colonial American could have viewed China as a botanical and zoological wonderland, as a utopia, or as a decaying despotic empire. (Awareness of Japan as a distinct nation with a distinct culture developed later than awareness of China, and mainly through Dutch sources. Dutchmen maintained the only Western ties with Japan.)

From Marco Polo onward, trade with Asia and its effects were important to European and subsequently American ideas of Asian culture. The Portuguese, then the Dutch, and finally the British brought cargoes of tea, silk, porcelain, and other exotic ware, which resulted in great profits for the Western merchants. And as one would suspect, the high cost of Oriental goods led to deliberate European attempts at imitation. Repeated failure, however, resulted from European attempts to produce true porcelain. The necessary combination of clays, admixtures, and glazing and firing techniques eluded Europeans until 1700 when Johann Böttger exhibited a product that could justly be called porcelain. His discoveries relieved Europe from total dependence on imports from China. During this same period, European artists developed what is known as Chinoiserie. Chinoiserie was a style of ornamentation that represented an Occidental interpretation of China with no real understanding of the aesthetics or philosophy behind Chinese art. A corresponding but lesser known development was known as Japonaiserie.

5

American colonial newspapers carried such advertisements as: "Whereas John Waghorne has lately Receiv'd fresh parcel of materials for the new Method of Japaning [sic], which was Invented in France for the Amusement and Benefit of the Ladies, and is now practised by most of the Quality and Gentry in Great Britain, with the greatest Satisfaction; . . ." [1] The advertisement captures the flavor of Japonaiserie. It was European, an amusement for the upper classes, and superficial.

Direct American contact with East Asia was unlikely during the colonial period because of the trade monopoly of the British East India Company. That company supplied the colonists with porcelain, nankeen cloth (a hand-loomed, sturdy cotton fabric), silk, cassia (a less expensive spice of the cinnamon family), furniture, and tea. The Chinese produced most of these items especially for export, which meant to a standard of taste and quality different from that available to and preferred by Chinese. American buyers and British sellers naturally assumed that they were handling authentic Chinese wares—porcelain produced, silks woven, and tea processed for Chinese. Although this was not the result of conscious deception, it led to misunderstanding. For many decades few Westerners could have ascertained the nature and quality of these items, and even the direct trade that resulted from American independence brought no new awareness.

Independence and the peace settlement of 1783 led both to crisis and to opportunity for American shippers and merchants in the China trade. The British declared old markets such as those in the British West Indies closed to American traders. However, independence meant that Americans need not recognize any monopoly of the East India Company. Legally, nothing stood in the way of direct trade with the Orient; minimizing the great obstacles, American traders quickly sought the new possibilities. In 1784 the *Empress of China* left New York harbor, its destination Canton. The ship's successful return in May of 1785 heralded the start of United States and Chinese trading relations. A 30 percent return on the capital invested was enough to assure continued effort. Numerous other Atlantic mercantile communities quickly joined the trade. In spite of domestic inhibitions such as the American Embargo of 1807–1809 and foreign difficulties caused by the Napoleonic Wars, some four hundred American vessels reached Canton between 1784 and 1812.* Their return cargoes sold readily in American markets.

Although after independence Americans on American ships conducted their own trade with China, much remained the same; old patterns and rules endured. In 1786 the American Continental Congress appointed Samuel Shaw, who had sailed as supercargo on the *Empress of China,* to the first consular position established in the Orient—consul at Canton, without salary. For the next fifty years consuls, chosen from the merchant community in East Asia, were the only permanent American spokesmen in China, and their paramount interest was trade. Shaw remarked in his journal that the Chinese had difficulty differentiating between Americans and Englishmen. The appearance of Americans in China created little concern and the Chinese made no adjustments beyond allowing American participation in existing commercial arrangements.

Upon arriving in China, American traders encountered the "Canton System." This term denoted the rules and regulations that the Chinese had evolved over years of trading with the Portuguese, the Dutch, and the British. American traders learned the system quickly and accepted its limits with alacrity. The profits were worth the hardships.

Regulations narrowly defined a trader's role in the Canton trade. An American ship first stopped at Macao, the Portuguese

---

* During the Wars of the French Revolution and Napoleon, 1793–1815, British and French pressures on neutral carrying trade, in which Americans were prominent, threatened to embroil the United States in war with one or both of those powers. Both Britain and France employed technical legal devices to justify seizure of ships trading with the enemy. As one way to avoid direct conflict with the European powers, President Thomas Jefferson in 1807 imposed an embargo on American shipping, in effect forbidding ships to sail for British or French ports, or other ports affected by the war rules and decrees of the contending powers in Europe. The embargo failed and ultimately was terminated.

outpost, where any Western women disembarked. Macao was the only place in China where a Western woman might stay. At Macao a captain hired a pilot to assure safe passage up the Pearl River to Whampoa. Because the river was too shallow for a deep-draft vessel to proceed farther upstream, the captain would anchor his ship at Whampoa among vessels from around the world. An actual floating city met the eye, a polyglot people desirous of profits from the China trade. Traders often remained at Whampoa and made arrangements for selling and buying cargo through Chinese agents, known as *compradors,* who exhibited varying ability, honesty, and cooperation. One shipmaster from Salem, Massachusetts, described a Chinese agent as "an honorable scoundrel," and one who would "tell you how much and why, and wherefore he cheats you." [2] Few Americans left descriptions so flattering.

Some traders journeyed on to Canton and encountered further restrictions. In Canton Westerners could move freely only in the immediate vicinity of the *Co-hong* factories—warehouses with living quarters above—located outside the Chinese city and along the riverbank.* A selected number of Chinese merchants licensed to trade with the barbarians—a label supplied to all non-Chinese—rented these facilities to Western merchants for the trading season. The rest of the year had to be spent in Macao. The factories at Canton and Macao were the Westerners' world in China.

Intellectual as well as physical restrictions hindered understanding. Americans and Chinese communicated in pidgin English. None of the early American merchants spoke Chinese, and none of the early Chinese agents spoke English. Peculiar nicknames abounded on both sides. The Chinese referred to one Western merchant as "the iron-headed old rat." Westerners called one Chinese "Tom Bull." It is not clear whether these

---

* The *Co-hong* was a guild of merchants licensed by and responsible to government officials to handle trade with Westerners. The term is from the Chinese *kung-hang,* meaning "officially authorized merchants." (See Yen-p'ing Hao, *The Comprador in Nineteenth Century China,* Cambridge, Mass., 1970.)

names had special meanings or were the result of accident. Chinese workers at the factories, believing their lives at stake, feared to teach their language. As a result, Americans like all other Westerners were cut off from the greater society around them. Occasional departures from this pattern meant little. Dinner in the home of a Chinese merchant provided no great understanding when neither host nor guest spoke the other's language. Pidgin English and the sequestered life at the factories were conducive to nothing but trade.

The physical restrictions on Westerners led to further confusion. Western traders could not visit sources of supply for the items they sought. Well into the nineteenth century Westerners believed that two distinct plants supplied green and black teas respectively. After China permitted Western travel and exploration, merchants discovered that processing caused the difference in tea. When Westerners did witness production methods, the impressions were not always favorable. James Morrow, a member of Matthew Perry's Japan expedition, recorded his horror after visiting a tea-processing establishment in the Canton area. He wrote that local Chinese kept their used tea leaves, dried them, and sold them to the factory, which then incorporated them into the export tea. Mr. Morrow's experience aside, had traders been allowed to visit the sources of production they would have marveled at the extent of job specialization, assembly line-like organization, and scale of operations at some sites. The porcelain center Ching-te Chen, although in decline during the nineteenth century, still produced great quantities of excellent porcelain. Visitors might have noticed also that the finest porcelain, as with the best of almost everything else, was not for export.

Perhaps the Chinese judged that the time was not right to dispel Western confusion of this sort. American buyers might have rejected the best in porcelain and other products through inability to appreciate its worth. To use decorative motifs on porcelain as an example, there was no way for the American to understand that the plum blossom sometimes signified sexual love; the bat, regal happiness; the iris, young female beauty and early summer; and the "three friends"—the pine tree, bamboo, and flowering plum—the qualities hoped for in a full masculine life: fortitude, pliability, and sexual vigor.[3] Rather than confront a new decorative symbolism, Americans followed the practice established by Europeans before them; they demanded porcelain decorated with Western motifs. Examples in museums and historic homes show a great quantity of American patriotic symbols, nautical emblems, and monograms or ciphers on imported porcelain. Although the surviving evidence is much less voluminous, a similar situation seems to have prevailed in silk and wallpapers. These obstacles to cultural appreciation led one student of the early nineteenth-century China trade to doubt whether any Yankee ship captain ever returned to New England with an authentic Chinese *objet d'art*.

Towns from Salem, Massachusetts, to Norfolk, Virginia, contain homes of early merchants and ship captains that offer a glimpse of East Asian influences. Many homes had a "Sunday box" containing toys and games for the subdued entertainment and amusement suitable for a Sunday afternoon. Inside the boxes were miniature carved ivory trinkets, checkers, chessmen, and the like. Owners commonly displayed porcelain, tea caddies, and lacquer ware. But excepting the ubiquitous porcelain, none of these items were necessities nor rose above the superficial; they were curiosities. Not displayed now are the durable and commonly worn trousers made from yellowish-brown nankeen cloth, nor the jars of cassia, nor even the tea, which headed the import lists. The trousers long since worn out, the cassia and tea consumed, the less ordinary items remain with us.

Curious and mundane though these trade items might have been, they were important to American merchants, so important that a compelling search resulted for goods to exchange with the Chinese. To satisfy the fancies of Chinese elites, Americans explored Pacific waters in search of seal and sea otter. Pacific furs and pelts, Hawaiian sandalwood, and New England ginseng each had their season, but the search led finally to opium. The fruit of the poppy ended the Westerner's need to pay for Chinese goods with scarce specie, and many American merchants became involved deeply in the opium trade. Chinese law forbade opium imports, but profits were such that widespread illicit traffic in the drug was common.

Through desire for trade, American opium dealers contributed to China's internal problems, and to an American image of the Chinese as decadent, demoralized, and deceitful, but not to development of cross-cultural understanding. Direct contact between Chinese and Americans in America failed to create an alternative view. The extensive shipping contact between East and West during the first half of the nineteenth century led only occasionally to Chinese reaching Atlantic ports. Reports cite one early Chinese who became a United States citizen. Some traders brought back Chinese servants. But seamen, servants, or citizens, they were few in number and left no lasting imprint.

For a while, a small school in Cornwall, Connecticut, seemed to promise cross-cultural development. The school, formally opened in 1817, hoped to educate American Indians and Hawaiians primarily but enrolled Greeks, Hindus, and Chinese also. In 1818 a New York merchant sent Wong Arce (!) from Canton to the school. Disobedience and immorality, it is said, led to his dismissal. Ah Lum and Ah Lan, from Philadelphia, had similar experiences. The school closed in 1827 as a result of marriages between two Cherokee Indian students and two girls from town.

Beyond the immediate trading community, East Asian influence on American life during the years between 1785 and 1850 was slight and, with few exceptions, might best be characterized as curiosity or novelty rather than trend. A brief look at architecture reveals that few builders attempted designs influenced by Chinese models. Certain homes had rooms with "Chinese trim," others incorporated the style known as Chinese Chippendale, still others followed designs of British builders. At best, and to a generous critic, these examples might fall into the category of Chinoiserie. One early home that contained a Chinese construction technique provided exception. A Dutch East India Company employee who had become an American citizen built a home at Croyden, outside of Philadelphia, during the 1790s. The home, known as China's Retreat, appeared to incorporate no other Chinese structural or design feature except a Chinese-style cupola on the roof. However, close inspection revealed that the windows were double leaves that slid into pockets in the walls, similar to screens in Chinese homes. Surviving records show no further use of such window treatment and China's Retreat remained an oddity. Surviving sketches and written descriptions of numerous buildings prove that Americans failed to grasp Chinese ideas and uses of space and form and ignored Asian construction methods. The buildings that used Oriental touches merely added small decorative embellishments to an otherwise Occidental plan and structure.

When given rare opportunity, Americans enjoyed displays of Oriental artifacts as they would any novelty. In 1838 Philadelphia was the site of an Oriental exhibition, probably the first in the United States. Nathan Dunn, a merchant and collector in that city, promoted an exhibition including a large collection of Chinese artifacts. Some of these were gathered by a Philadelphia trader, W. W. Wood, the rest by Dunn. The collection included life-sized figures in native costumes, models of streets and houses, and examples of Chinese manufacture and handicraft. Reports of the event indicate public enthusiasm, but three years later the sheriff sold the building and its contents on account of debt. The new owner shipped the collection to Europe and what became of the artifacts thereafter remains a mystery. The exact nature, authenticity, and quality of the exhibit are also obscure.

Had a visitor to the Dunn exposition wished to undertake scholarly inquiry into Chinese culture, rather than simply to gaze at novelties, formidable obstacles would have arisen. Some American communities did have East Asian collections. Ralph Waldo Emerson, for example, used the Harvard Library, the Boston Athenaeum collection, and books from the personal library of Henry Wadsworth Longfellow to satisfy his interest in Oriental philosophy and culture. The writings of the Jesuit fathers of the seventeenth and eighteenth centuries were available in French. In English, works published by missionary presses at Malacca and Serampore in Indonesia and elsewhere in Southeast Asia offered variations on those narratives written by British merchants and diplomats. Memories of American ship captains, merchants, and early diplomats gave an American flavor. There were also one or two translations of Chinese dramas and novels in American libraries. However, in that substantial shelf on China, various problems remained. The Jesuit works over-idealized China, the eighteenth-century British over-criticized China, the American works drew only on the Canton experience, the missionary works contained their own bias, and the translations were faulty. Excepting the Jesuits and the Chinese, few authors of these written accounts were competent in the Chinese language. A mid-century scholar could not delve too deeply into the unfamiliar affairs and ways of China or Japan.

Samuel Wells Williams, an American missionary-scholar-diplomat who spent much of his life in China, labored to overcome obstacles of Western ignorance. On a press available at Canton, he printed *Easy Lessons in Chinese* in 1841. Its distribution, he hoped, would render unnecessary the continued use of pidgin English. *Easy Lessons* went through several printings and revisions. Still, a writer for the *North American Review* identified one of the book's problems when he questioned the use of the word "easy" in the title.

Some of Williams' further contributions to knowledge of China were the result of hard work and good friends. He returned to the United States on furlough in 1845 after thirteen years in China. While in this country he prepared a series of lectures on the social life, history, and institutions of China, hoping to raise money for a new font of movable Chinese type. He delivered more than a hundred lectures over the next two years. He then decided to rework the lectures and to attempt publication of a study that he described as something between an encyclopedia and a primer. He wanted to change the minds of those Americans who believed that seriousness on the subject of China was preposterous. He hoped also to increase interest in evangelizing China. Although there were few serious books on China available, Williams nearly failed to secure publication. Only after two friends of Williams' guaranteed Wiley & Putnam against any losses did the firm agree in 1848 to set *The Middle Kingdom* in print. The finished product remained the standard work on China for decades.

In another sense, Williams' experience presents an example of the ambivalence common among Americans exposed to East Asian culture. His long years in China, coupled with his achievements linguistic and literary, led him to great sympathy for the Chinese. Yet Williams, under stress, wrote:

> It is much easier loving the souls of the heathen in the abstract than in the concrete encompassed as they are in such dirty bodies, speaking forth their foul language and vile natures exhibiting every evidence of depravity.[4]

Apparently, familiarity led not only to understanding but to contempt.

During the first seventy-odd years of direct American-Chinese relations several changes occurred to influence cultural association via trade and travel. Around 1800 the United States had been a rural society unable to meet its own needs and desires. East Asia supplied goods not produced in the United States because of technological or geographical limitations. But by 1850 the United States stood on the threshold of widespread industrialization (and parts of Europe were already industrialized). This accounts for the fact that American importation of Chinese goods changed in character. By mid-century, American importation of tea amounted to almost 80 percent by value of all East Asian goods. American and European sources had replaced the demand for silk and nankeen. European and American suppliers provided porcelain and porcelain substitutes at a price and style more attractive to American buyers. Technological advances had caused the United States to rely less upon China for manufactures, and so tea, unavailable in Europe and America, remained the major import.

Development in Asia at mid-century, as in America, seemed

to point in new directions. The 1840s witnessed British success in breaking the Canton System. Settlement of the Opium War expanded relations between Western nations and China. The American-engineered opening of Japan soon augmented the British achievement. Eventually the new relationships resulted in numerous Chinese workers temporarily working in the United States and Americans temporarily residing in China. The impact of the Chinese immigrants was slight. In turn, the merchants, missionaries, diplomats, naval officers, tourists, and students with experience in the Orient spread little East Asian influence in the United States. For most Americans, exposure to China and Japan proved of little consequence; convinced of Western superiority, whether technological or racial or moral, they went to teach, not to learn. For a few, however, the Orient represented new ideas and a chance to expand Western cultural horizons. Unfortunately, because these pioneers encountered few public and private institutional vehicles—agencies to spread ideas and processes—the impact of the cultural pioneers was less than it might have been.

The arrival of large numbers of Chinese on the Pacific coast did little to increase American appreciation of the Chinese or their culture. Work in the mining country and in railway construction during the 1850s brought thousands of Chinese sojourners to the West Coast. As sojourners, they intended to be in the United States only temporarily—until they had saved sufficient money to return to China and lift their families out of poverty. As sojourners, they came mainly from the peasantry—unlikely carriers of sophisticated artistic or philosophical accomplishment. As sojourners, they kept to themselves, refused acculturation, competed for jobs, and aroused feelings of prejudice in Caucasian Americans. Their arts, crafts, and ceremonies stirred little interest in the American population. Citizens of the western states mingled with the Chinese, used their services, hired their labor, but benefited little from the association beyond developing a taste for Chinese cooking.

A few Americans who were open to new ideas journeyed to China and Japan. In the 1860s Henry Adams and his artist friend John La Farge traveled to Japan in search of inspiration, new truths, and, as La Farge quipped, nirvana. Neither Adams nor La Farge found the Buddhist paradise, nor even new truths, but La Farge did find direct inspiration. He found the landscapes of Japan suggestive of the miraculous, and their representations later graced the walls of the Church of the Ascension in New York. He painted other murals that bespoke Asian influence; Confucius appears on walls in Baltimore and St. Paul. As one of the foremost American designers of stained glass in the late nineteenth century, La Farge admitted substantial Japanese influence in his designs. To artists and art connoisseurs, La Farge was a propagandist for East Asia.

Another traveler was Ernest Fenollosa, whose legacy was of great importance. In 1878 he accepted appointment to an academic chair at the University of Tokyo. This Massachusetts scholar first met the Japanese at the height of their enthusiasm for the West. For a brief but dangerous time, extremists urged their fellow Japanese to discard much of their cultural heritage. The American worked to counter this trend and helped to preserve important Japanese works of art. At the same time he acquired a large Japanese art collection. Charles Weld purchased this collection and presented it to the Boston Museum of Fine Arts. In 1890 Fenollosa returned to the United States and became curator at that museum; in effect, he was in charge of his own collection. Fenollosa's contribution to American knowledge of East Asia came also from publications concerning art, poetry, and drama. Specialists remember him for *The Chinese Written Character as a Medium of Poetry; Epochs of Chinese and Japanese Art* and *Hiroshige, the Artist of Mist, Snow and Rain.* His interest in drama resulted in an unpublished manuscript on Nō drama. Ezra Pound later revised and published this work as *Certain Noble Plays of Japan.* These publications reached a narrow audience, but were, nevertheless, groundbreaking studies for the group of American poets who called themselves imagists and wrote in the early twentieth century.

But there could not be many people such as Fenollosa; except for missionaries and their children, few Americans could understand either Chinese or Japanese. Formal instruction in Asian languages at the better-known American colleges and universities did not begin until the 1870s. Only then did officials at Yale appoint their first professor of Chinese Language and Literature, and then never called upon him to offer instruction. During that same decade Harvard raised money to secure a native Chinese to teach his language for three years—to test the American demand.

Learned societies were slow in taking interest in East Asia. Founded in 1842, the American Oriental Society directed its energies and enthusiasms toward biblical and ancient Egyptian and Mesopotamian studies. Only at the end of the nineteenth century did a few members become active in the study of Chinese civilization. No other group organized for such study until the turn of the century.

Lack of knowledge about East Asia created practical problems for the American government. Negotiations with China and Korea to secure a commercial treaty with Korea in the early 1880s reveal confusion among scholars and political leaders regarding fundamental assumptions of Chinese foreign relations. Informed sources of the day maintained that Korea was either independent or dependent on China. This uncertainty extended to the United States Department of State. And, if Korea was a dependency, no one knew what the dependency entailed. The naval officer in charge of negotiations, Commodore Robert W. Shufeldt, ultimately resolved the issue. He secured a Korean-American treaty that contained no mention of dependency. However, the Korean king sent a letter to the American President stating that although Korea handled its own foreign and domestic affairs, his country was a dependency of China.

Confusion flourished also in areas of the natural sciences, where botany illustrates the limits of American interest. During the 1850s Charles Wright, a former surveyor from Texas, roamed the Hong Kong area and collected dried plant specimens which included more than five hundred species. Wright's work led to the 1861 publication of George Bentham's *Flora Hongkongensis,* and Wright became associated with the Gray

Herbarium at Harvard. Another botanist, James Morrow, accompanied the Perry Expedition to Japan in the 1850s; he labored under almost impossible conditions to secure plants and seeds from Japan and China. To his disappointment, he saw most of the live specimens perish on the sea voyages. A few plants survived the arduous transit and reached Washington, D.C. There, gardeners placed them in greenhouses near the Capitol and maintained them as spectacles. Seeds sent to the United States by Morrow went to various fanciers around the country. In mid-century, the United States Patent Office sponsored more than three hundred stores from which foreign and domestic seeds of an unusual nature were distributed to those interested. However, there was no systematic testing and distribution until the end of the century when David Fairchild took charge at the Department of Agriculture's Section of Seed and Plant Introduction.

What was lacking in the United States was present in Great Britain. There, several companies sent collectors to East Asia in search of new and marketable plants. English gardens of the nineteenth century made such enterprises profitable. Neither the great gardens nor their suppliers existed in the United States; and Americans interested in Oriental plants sent to Britain for camellias, azaleas, rhododendrons, and chrysanthemums. Interest and sponsorship by the Arnold Arboretum of Harvard, the Field Museum in Chicago, and the Department of Agriculture were far in the future; their efforts began in earnest only after the turn of the century.

No Asian plant had a more curious history in America than the soybean. A victim of geographical, professional, and institutional shortcomings, the soybean had first arrived in the United States when Benjamin Franklin sent some seeds from France in the late eighteenth century. A Philadelphia-published encyclopedia of 1804 announced that the soybean would grow in Pennsylvania and was well worth cultivating. Seventy-five years of disinterest followed. Then in the 1880s, C. C. Georgeson, a Kansas researcher, brought seeds from Japan and experimented with their cultivation in Kansas. Their failure in the windswept Kansas landscape led to another dead end. American farmers had to wait until systematic testing and collecting in the 1920s produced strains suitable for American soils and climate. From there, it was a straight line toward the soybean becoming one of America's main crops.

Because Americans were slow to develop methods to extend understanding of Oriental culture, it was fortunate that the Japanese gave this country a push. In the 1870s American organizers invited various countries to participate in the Philadelphia Centennial Exposition. The Japanese government responded affirmatively. Fifty carloads of construction materials and items for display subsequently arrived in Philadelphia. In addition, Japanese workmen came from Japan to assemble a pavilion and a teahouse-bazaar combination. These buildings afforded Americans their first opportunity to view authentic Japanese structures.[5]

Interest in the Japanese pavilion at Philadelphia, coupled with the research of Edward Morse, resulted in American builders and architects having reliable information about Japanese techniques and styles. Although some technical journals had published articles on various aspects of Japanese building, in 1886 the most important work appeared. In that year Morse published *Japanese Homes and Their Surroundings*. Morse, like his fellow citizen of Salem, Fenollosa, had journeyed to Japan and taught at the University of Tokyo. While in Japan Morse became a collector of ceramics and a student of Japanese homes, all before the Japanese were exposed to Western influence. Morse illustrated his work profusely and supplemented it with much detailed information, so that his book dominated the field for more than fifty years.

Another Japanese pavilion graced the Chicago-based World's Columbian Exposition of 1893. The pavilions at the two fairs and Morse's book inspired a generation of American architects. Frank Lloyd Wright, who worked in Chicago at the turn of the century, remarked that he saw the Japanese home as a "supreme study in elimination . . . of the insignificant." [6] Wright strove to reject the confused, the trivial, and the insignificant in his designs. He acknowledged freely and repeatedly his debt to Japan. The visually simplified, more straightforward designs of mid-twentieth-century American builders are partly the result of such influence.

East Asian exhibits at that first American centennial exposition at Philadelphia affected the American ceramics industry also. The pottery on display attracted the attention of George Ward Nichols and his wife, Maria Longworth Nichols. In 1877 Mr. Nichols published *Art Education Applied to Industry,* in which he predicted that Japanese and Chinese exhibits at the fair would "exert a wide and positive influence upon American industries." [7] Mrs. Nichols was instrumental in fulfilling her husband's prophecy. During the 1870s she had experimented with pottery decoration and glazes, and in 1880 her father provided money to establish a pottery. Thus began what was later called the Rookwood pottery, one of the most artistically successful potteries in the United States. A record book describes the first two hundred pieces produced at Mrs. Nichols' pottery. Among the descriptions are many that attribute inspiration to Japanese sources in shape, use, or decoration. At Rookwood the Japanese influence ran even deeper. In 1887 Kataro Shirayamadani joined the staff as a decorator.* In 1893 the management sent him to visit potteries in Japan to discover if Japanese techniques could solve problems encountered at Rookwood. Although no record survives to state Shirayamadani's findings, the attempted cross-cultural exchange is significant. Through the years Japanese and Chinese designs appeared regularly on Rookwood products. Their success and prestige was such that other potteries followed their lead in style and technique.

Today it is almost inconceivable that by 1900, after well over a hundred years of trading in East Asia, after decades of travel

---

* The name is given as it appears in the book on the Rookwood pottery, cited below. The first syllable is irregular according to the name rules promulgated during the Meiji period; the final vowel should probably be a double syllable. But some such anomalies were residual for years after the reforms. It is also possible that the name was distorted when the artist came to America.

there, and after thousands of Chinese and Japanese had immigrated to the United States, most Americans nevertheless remained uninformed about Oriental culture. To be sure, limited Japanese and Chinese influences have shown in such things as American pottery, architecture, and literature. But throughout the nineteenth century American exposure to the Far East led to superficial understanding only. In part, this lack of depth is traceable to restrictions placed on Westerners in Asia until mid-century and beyond. In part Americans share responsibility for their superficiality. Increasing technological superiority in the United States made Eastern methods and techniques seem less necessary or desirable. Convinced of their moral and racial superiority, most Americans believed that there was little to learn in the Far East. Americans who did wish to learn from the Orient found the way strewn with obstacles. The lack of American educational opportunities to learn about China and Japan meant that only the most persevering could achieve expertise in Asian culture.

American interest in Oriental culture remained fragmented, partial, and unsynthesized throughout the nineteenth century. Those few individuals receptive to East Asian cultural influences lived, taught, and propagandized virtually alone, isolated from supportive groups. Organizations that might have served as cohesive and coherent centers of cultural exchange lay in the future. Missionaries and merchants were the only groups capable of influencing opinion and, perhaps, policy, but their goals often differed from one another. Thus early Sino-American cultural contact left an imprint both modest and ambiguous.

Notes

[1] George Francis Dow, *The Arts and Crafts in New England, 1704–1755* (Topsfield, Mass., 1927; reprint ed., New York, 1967), p. 266.

[2] Quoted in Jean McClure Mudge, *Chinese Export Porcelain for the American Trade, 1785–1835* (Newark, Del., 1962), p. 28.

[3] Philip Rawson, *Introducing Oriental Art* (New York, 1973), p. 18.

[4] Frederick W. Williams, *Life and Letters of Samuel Wells Williams* (New York, 1889), p. 174.

[5] A cast-iron pagoda attracted less attention. American enthusiasm for Chinese or pseudo-Chinese influence had waned since early in the century.

[6] Quoted in Clay Lancaster, *The Japanese Influence in America* (New York, 1963), p. 88.

[7] Quoted in Herbert Peck, *The Book of Rookwood Pottery* (New York, 1968), p. 4.

Readings and Sources

Barth, Gunther, *Bitter Strength: A History of the Chinese in the United States, 1850–1870* (Cambridge, Mass., 1964). An impressive introduction to the topic. Barth gives an excellent account of life in the Canton delta, the region from which most Chinese immigrants came.

Camp, Wendell H., *The World in Your Garden* (Washington, D.C., 1957). Although written for the general audience, this work contains valuable information about plant migration and plant exploration.

Chisolm, Lawrence W., *Fenollosa: The Far East and American Culture* (New Haven, 1963). This is the definitive biography of Ernest Fenollosa, citizen of Salem, Massachusetts, sojourner in Japan, contributor to American understanding of China and Japan.

Christy, Arthur, ed., *The Asian Legacy and American Life* (New York, 1942). This volume contains many valuable insights into cultural borrowing by Americans. America's debt to Asian agriculture is especially well documented.

Cole, Allan B., *A Scientist with Perry in Japan* (Chapel Hill, N.C., 1947). An important biography of James Morrow, who accompanied Matthew C. Perry on the mid-century expedition to open Japan to the West. The trials endured by Morrow in the name of science are described in an interesting way.

Cox, D. H. M., *Plant Hunting in China* (London, 1945). This study concentrates on efforts of British botanical explorers but does mention some Americans.

Danton, George H., *The Culture Contacts of the United States and China* (New York, 1931). This is one of the earliest works to discuss Chinese influences in the United States.

Dennett, Tyler, *Americans in Eastern Asia* (New York, 1963, reprint of New York, 1922, edition). Although dated, Dennett's study is important for any investigation of official encounters between Americans and Orientals in the nineteenth century.

Dulles, Foster Rhea, *The Old China Trade* (Boston, 1930). This book is worth consulting for early American diplomatic and commercial relations.

Edwardes, Michael, *East-West Passage: The Travel of Ideas, Arts and Inventions Between Asia and the Western World* (New York, 1971). Edwardes writes of European rather than American experiences, but his insights apply in either case.

Honour, Hugh, *Chinoiserie: The Vision of Cathay* (London, 1961). Written essentially about Europe, this book has both direct and indirect relevance for the United States.

Iriye, Akira, *Across the Pacific: An Inner History of American-East Asian Relations* (New York, 1967). Iriye deals with the images that Americans and East Asians have had of one another through their long association.

Lancaster, Clay, *The Japanese Influence in America* (New York, 1963). This book emphasizes architecture, design, and the applied arts.

Lee, Rose Hum, *The Chinese in the United States of America* (Hong Kong, 1960). One of three or four standard works on the assimilation difficulties encountered by Chinese immigrants, Lee's book discusses American perceptions of the Chinese also.

Lee, W. Storrs, *The Yankees of Connecticut* (New York, 1957). This volume is one of many local histories that describe the impact of the Orient on New England towns and states.

Miller, Stuart C., *The Unwelcome Immigrants: The American Image of the Chinese, 1785–1882* (Berkeley, Calif., 1969). Miller presents the thesis that American prejudice against the Chinese was deep-seated in nineteenth-century society, of early origin, and national in scope.

Morison, Samuel E., *The Maritime History of Massachusetts* (Boston, 1921). Morison's excellent volume is required reading for understanding the role of Massachusetts in early American trade with China.

Mudge, Jean McClure, *Chinese Export Porcelain for the American Trade, 1785–1835* (Newark, Del., 1962). Books on porcelain exist in great abundance, but the best remains the Mudge volume.

Neumann, William L., *America Encounters Japan: From Perry to MacArthur* (Baltimore, 1963). Although Neumann primarily analyzes the ideas and attitudes that have shaped United States foreign policy, he includes evidence of Asian influences on the American population.

Peck, Herbert, *The Book of Rookwood Pottery* (New York, 1968). This book is a full and detailed account of the birth, rise to prominence, and demise of Rookwood.

Schwantes, Robert, *Japanese and Americans: A Century of Cultural Relations* (New York, 1955). Here is a useful study of Japanese-American relations.

Williams, Frederick Wells, *The Life and Letters of Samuel Wells Williams* (New York, 1889). This biography contains a great deal of important information about China at mid-nineteenth century.

The following museums contain the more famous American collections of East Asian art: the Freer Gallery of Art, Washington, D.C.; the Metropolitan Museum, New York; the Museum of Fine Arts, Boston; the Peabody Museum, Salem, Mass.; the University Museum of Philadelphia; and the William Rockhill Nelson Gallery, Kansas City, Mo.

Chapter Two

Chinese in America: The Nineteenth-Century Experience

BY FREDERICK B. HOYT AND EUGENE P. TRANI

Beginning late in the 1840s, Chinese immigration to the West Coast of the United States introduced into Sino-American relations long-enduring uncertainties and confusions as American domestic reactions spilled over into foreign affairs. Journalists such as Horace Greeley underscored American fears of a yellow peril by predicting that the "rivulet" of Chinese would, if unchecked, swell to a Niagara. Greeley also prescribed a remedy to foreclose that possibility—prohibition of further Chinese immigration. The Exclusion Act of 1882 lessened some American uneasiness concerning the new and growing Chinese community in the United States, although in both relative and absolute terms Chinese immigration to America was never more than a trickle. The total of Chinese in the United States peaked at 108,000 in 1890; this number was not equaled again until after World War II. Natural attrition—some Chinese died and others returned to the Celestial Kingdom—reduced the Chinese population in the United States to around 70,000 by 1910, a figure that remained fairly constant through the first four decades of the twentieth century. Despite these modest numbers, however, the effects of Chinese immigration to the United States were of substantial interest and influence in ensuing years.

Chinese arrived in the United States uncertain about what to expect. Most Chinese came as temporary residents, as sojourners. Their purpose was to acquire wealth and to return as quickly as possible to the Middle Kingdom, where they could retire as wealthy gentlemen amid familiar surroundings. Initially welcomed to work the mines and build the railroads, the Chinese found themselves objects of riots once the mines were worked out and the railroads completed. They resolved their own uncertainties by retreating into the cities of the West, especially San Francisco. Thus were born the Chinatowns, the residences of most Chinese until the emergence of a stable middle-class Chinese-American community and the relaxation of white racial attitudes permitted dispersal in the 1940s and 1950s.

The Exclusion Act of 1882 ended racial uncertainty; it also left a residual confusion regarding Chinese family life in the United States. Originally viewing their stay in the United States as short-term, Chinese men left their wives behind to guard the ancestral hearth and to serve as hostages for the repayment of money they had borrowed for passage. As a result, the emigrants from China were predominantly male. Even during the height of unrestricted immigration to the United States, fewer than 8 percent of Chinese immigrants were women. The Exclusion Act of 1882 further restricted entry of Chinese women into the United States. A sexual balance in the Chinese-American population, essential to the rise of a stable American-born Chinese community, did not appear until after American immigration laws were relaxed during World War II.

The Almost Welcome Immigrant: The Initial Reception

Racial tension was latent in the differing value structures Americans and Chinese brought to their encounter in the United States; their previous contact in China had virtually ensured the Chinese of an uncertain reception. However, conflict was at best a subordinate theme in the experience of the Chinese in America from their appearance in the late 1840s until the early 1870s. Disturbed conditions in China outweighed cultural and legal restrictions against Chinese emigration, while the economic need for Chinese labor on the West Coast enabled Americans to subdue their own negative images of the Chinese.

The cost of immigration was potentially high for Chinese, because traditional Chinese values were sharply at variance from those held by most Americans. Steeped in Confucian thought, Chinese started with the premise that propriety and personal relationships were more important than the individualism that characterized Americans. The hierarchical society of traditional China dictated deferential obedience by the lower classes in return for the paternalistic protection offered by the elite. The rigidity of the system reminded many Americans of slavery. The Chinese view of government also differed markedly from American ideas. In China, good government depended on having an emperor who acted like an emperor. Americans, on the other hand, extolled democratic institutions, which placed impartial laws above the whims of individuals. In the historical record of Sino-foreign contact, aliens had traditionally adopted Chinese values, even when the Middle Kingdom had been ruled by "barbarians" for hundreds of years. Americans, by contrast, assumed that immigrants to the United States would become absorbed into the American mainstream.

Obstacles other than conflicting cultural values confronted a potential Chinese émigré. He would have to leave the psychological security and physical presence of his family. A decision to emigrate would also cut across the traditional Chinese view of the world, which held that the Middle Kingdom was the sole repository of civilization. Departure meant defiance of the Manchu government, which formally proscribed emigration until 1890. Finally, the trip to the United States required a heavy expenditure and a commitment to work until the money was repaid, usually a long-term arrangement. The most common system for financing the voyage was the credit-ticket arrangement, in which a Chinese broker advanced passage. Collection was then assigned to so-called companies in the United States—clan guilds dominated by merchants. Until the debt was repaid, the Chinese laborer was subject to discipline and control of the guild. Workers who attempted prematurely to break their obligation placed themselves in jeopardy, for collusion between Chinese creditors and shippers prevented Chinese who were still in debt from returning to their homeland. Small wonder that Gunther Barth has called the credit-ticket system "partly a disguised slave trade." [1]

Notwithstanding the uncertain perils of emigration, intense pressures within China caused more than 100,000 Chinese to leave for the United States. For the Middle Kingdom in general, the prosperity of the early years of Manchu rule had contributed to a spectacular population growth. The census reports of the 1650s counted approximately 150 million Chinese. In the next two centuries, the population doubled. This increase, without a corresponding improvement in agricultural production, strained the resources of China and impoverished the peasantry.

Population pressure, a typical indication of dynastic decline, became especially pronounced in south China. Long a stronghold of opposition to the Manchu dynasty, that region experienced particular problems. Through Canton, the first major entrepôt of European trade, precious metals drained from the interior to pay for the increasing imports of opium. The opening of treaty ports in central China, and particularly the financial and commercial displacement of Canton by Shanghai after the Anglo-Chinese treaty of Nanking in 1842, further dislocated the economy of south China. Peasant unrest then combined with distorted Christian teaching to produce the Taiping Rebellion. Beginning in south China in the early 1850s, the uprising devastated much of China south of the Yangtze and took nearly 30 million lives before it was extinguished in the mid-1860s. As a result of these difficulties, news of the discovery of gold in California in 1848 was as welcome in Canton and Hong Kong as in New York and Chicago, for the American West offered more than gold to certain Chinese. Short of unskilled labor, the underdeveloped West offered jobs.

From the American side, negative reports by Americans in China left their countrymen uncertain that the Chinese could be desirable immigrants. For more than half a century, businessmen, missionaries, and diplomats had commented critically on Chinese people and customs, emphasizing incompatible or, from the American perspective, undesirable traits. As the dream of selling American products to 400 million Chinese turned to chimera by the middle of the nineteenth century, embittered merchants attributed failure to everything from insufficient military force to the devious business practices of the Chinese. An entrepreneur, for example, theorized that the large sleeves in the flowing Chinese gowns were designed to aid in theft. The notion of Chinese as crafty and unscrupulous traders preceded the appearance of Chinese in the United States. Protestant missionaries contributed equally unflattering pictures of heathens who steadfastly refused to repudiate Confucius for Christ. One evangelist bitterly measured the distance between the Christian teacher and the Confucian scholar: "To publish a book on science or religion is to insult them [the learned Chinese], for in doing that you take for granted that China is not the depository of all truth and knowledge. . . . To propound progress is to insult them, for therein you intimate that China has not reached the acme of civilization, and that you stand on a higher platform than they do." [2] Out of frustration, as Stuart Creighton Miller has observed, the nineteenth-century missionaries prayed for the salvation of China by demanding that American military forces storm Satan's citadel and win the pagan land for Christ.[3] As a corollary, the ministers portrayed the Chinese as depraved heathens, whose atheism led them into every imaginable vice. Damning accounts by American and European diplomats reinforced the business and missionary condemnation of the Chinese as deceitful and egocentric. In short, Americans in China had conditioned the American public to an essentially negative view of the Chinese long before the first Chinese arrived in the United States.

Americans were not reassured by their initial contacts with the Chinese who came to the United States after 1848. The first large group of nonwhites to arrive voluntarily, the Chinese literally stepped off the boat into the controversy over slavery. The conditions of the credit-ticket system sharpened the comparisons rather than the contrasts. The organization of Chinese workers into gangs under overseers resembled the plantation slavery to which Californians had become increasingly sensitive. Though the state had entered the Union without slavery as part of the compromise of 1850, the "phantom of the Slave Power, conspiring to debase California to the level of a slave state, came to haunt Californians" for the remainder of the decade.[4] Further, the odors associated with the Chinese, and particularly Chinese cooking, so much criticized by Americans in China, offended Californians as well. As the historian Rodman W. Paul has observed, Americans believed the strange smells were due to the Chinese proclivity for cooking rats, a tenet that persisted at least until the 1930s.[5] Also, American reformers soon discovered evils peculiar to the Chinese community—widespread gambling, opium-smoking, and prostitution.

A temporary combination of circumstances, however, resolved the confusion attendant upon the arrival of the earliest Chinese immigrants. As residents of a new state, Californians were initially optimistic about their ability to absorb and transform all immigrants, even the Chinese. "It may not be many years before the halls of Congress are graced by the presence of a long-queued Mandarin, sitting, voting, and speaking beside a don from Santa Fe and a Kanaker from Hawaii," predicted the *Daily Alta Californian* in an 1851 editorial. "The 'China boys' will yet vote at the same polls, study at the same schools, and bow at the same altar as our own countrymen," the paper added.[6] The thought of the Chinese bowing "at the same altar" soon attracted missionaries from five American denominations.

William Speer, a Presbyterian clergyman, returned from Canton in 1853 to open the first church among the Chinese in San Francisco. "This early interest of Protestant clergymen in the Chinese in California," Robert Seager has noted, "was clearly related to their belief that God Himself had brought the Chinese to California to be Christianized." [7] Conversion along the West Coast appeared to provide a springboard for sending native converts back to China. Another evangelist, pointing to the proximity of California to the "teeming millions of Asia," urged Christians to pray for the conversion of China: "Let all the appliances of Gospel warfare be furnished and employed against this Sebastopol of Satan. Let it be stormed by the allied forces of King Immanuel, and very soon we will control the whole empire of darkness, and, under the banner of the Cross, will march to the conquest of the world." [8]

More important in arresting the uncertainties Americans entertained concerning the desirability of Chinese immigrants, however, was the need for labor in the underpopulated West. The Chinese promised to bring economic benefits to a society rich in land and resources, but poor in manpower. For a variety of American businessmen, such as the shippers in need of cargo for the return trip from China and the industrial barons who held mines and railroad grants, the Chinese were welcome immigrants indeed. They were disciplined, hardworking, organized, and not nearly as likely to run off in search of gold as white workers. As late as the 1860s, white Americans proved unreliable for the construction of railroads. Once the company transported them to the railhead, they tended to abandon the construction site and search for gold. In short, Chinese shared a common goal with American entrepreneurs: to make money as rapidly as possible. Nor did Chinese aspirations challenge white American workers, who found easier opportunities than service as a common laborer along the frontier. Chinese generally took the jobs that whites scorned. Chinese labor was complementary in another sense as well, for the predominantly male society of the American West was short of "womanpower." To reach their goal of accumulating money for a successful return to China, Chinese performed tasks American society has generally deemed "woman's work," particularly cooking and laundering.

In summary, Americans initially received the Chinese as an almost welcome immigrant, despite cultural differences and negative images. Racial tension added an uncertain dimension, to be sure. But it was latent as long as Americans remained socially optimistic, as long as the expanding economy continued to provide noncompetitive and subordinate openings for unskilled workers, and as long as the Chinese remained economically supplementary and complementary.

From Exploitation to Enclosure

Harmonious relations between Chinese and white Americans were generally short-lived in each of the major occupational categories that the Chinese filled; uncertainty returned in the form of hostility, conflict, and white control. The mining frontier—the original stimulus in attracting Chinese to California—determined the initial pattern of both Chinese settlement and the white response. Beginning with the gold mines of California, Chinese followed the extractive industries eastward, which eventually accounted for their presence in territories such as Wyoming, Nevada, and Montana. The size of the Chinese community in the mining camps frequently opened support and supply jobs for additional Chinese. In the towns that sprang up to service the camps, Chinese opened restaurants, noodle parlors, and laundries. But the amicable coexistence of whites and Chinese was as temporary as the existence of most mining communities. Increased mechanization and declining productivity both meant high unemployment, a situation that frequently produced riots as well as legislative restrictions on Chinese miners.

The same pattern—initial and mutual exploitation and temporary coexistence—developed in the second major occupational opportunity the West offered Chinese: the railroads, particularly the new transcontinental road, the Central Pacific. To encourage construction, Congress during the Civil War had empowered the Union Pacific to push westward from Omaha, and the Central Pacific to build east from San Francisco. Each railroad was promised funding in proportion to track laid, which put a premium on the speed of construction. While the Union Pacific, which hired Irish immigrants, was laying a mile of track a day, the Central Pacific was bogged down fifty miles from the point of origin two full years after inaugurating construction.

The problem for the Central Pacific was finding reliable workers. White laborers frequently vanished in the foothills to search for gold. Chinese brought in during 1865, according to legend as strikebreakers, proved so satisfactory that 3,000 were working for the railroad by the end of the year. After four more years, 80 percent of the labor force was Chinese. Though the company initially drew upon the pool of Chinese displaced from the mines, the Central Pacific sent recruiters to south China, where they eventually hired nearly 10,000 additional Chinese. Leland Stanford, president of the railroad and governor of California, later admitted that the Chinese were essential to the completion of the railroad. He might have had in mind the fact that they were far more docile than whites, since they were under the discipline of their gang foremen. The president might also have had in mind the greater expense the road would have incurred with white labor. The Central Pacific paid Chinese employees the same wages as whites, but did not provide the Chinese a similar allowance for room and board. The saving amounted to at least $30 per worker per month. Nor did the Central Pacific pay the Chinese extra for filling skilled or dangerous jobs.

As with the mines, work on the Central Pacific and on some of the other western railroads provided only a temporary basis for peaceful relations between Chinese and Americans. Once the roads were completed, the Chinese were forced again to search for employment as unskilled laborers. From railroads, the Chinese increasingly gravitated to general labor, especially jobs that still comprise their ethnic stereotype—menial labor, restaurants, and laundries. The vocational movement can be seen in the small but typical Chinese community in Nevada. Fifty Chinese entered the territory in the late 1860s to dig ditches, and nearly a thousand of their countrymen soon arrived to work the mines and build spur lines for the Central Pacific. With the completion of the railroads and the decline of workable mines, most Chinese sought greater economic opportunity in the larger urban centers in Nevada. By the 1870s, nearly half the Chinese in the state resided in Carson City or Virginia City, where most were unskilled laborers. Cooks and servants constituted the majority of the remainder. This emphasis on unskilled and service jobs held true even in the two major communities, where the size of the general population permitted some diversification.

The Nevada pattern reflected two facets of the changing Chinese experience in the United States that came to dominate relations between Chinese and white Americans. First, Chinese vocations were increasingly urban, which transformed the Chinatowns from temporary residences for temporary residents into permanent residences for permanent strangers. Second, the movement into subordinate positions in urban areas indicated a shift in the cost/benefit equation that had made the Chinese an almost welcome immigrant. The social cost of unskilled Chinese labor began to outweigh the benefits for significant and vociferous interest groups. The consequence of the change was an increasingly conscious policy to control and enclose the Chinese population, to control occupations and enclose Chinese in Chinatowns. The change was fraught with potential for violence.

The Chinese had been almost welcome immigrants so long as Americans believed the Chinese would become useful citizens and productive workers, but by the 1870s this assumption, or hope, was giving way to new uncertainties about the place of aliens in America. Thirty years of unrestricted immigration had produced no senators and few citizens, and federal legislation soon curtailed the immigration. An 1870 effort by abolitionist

Senator Charles Sumner had failed to link naturalization of Chinese with that of the newly freed black. The Exclusion Act of 1882, which forbade federal and state courts from conferring citizenship on Chinese, codified what had become general practice.

Americans who had initially welcomed the Chinese, such as the evangelists in San Francisco, began to defect from public support of the Oriental immigrants. Originally enthusiastic over the possibility of harvesting new souls and possibly replanting them in China, churchmen found the Chinese highly resistant. The schools they established for Chinese, to take an example, taught both English and Christian doctrine. But the Chinese divorced the language training from the message, and the record of conversion was as barren in the United States as in China. Despite the obvious pressures of living in a Christian environment, the proselytes, after twenty years of mission work, could claim only 680 Chinese Christians among the estimated 100,000 Chinese in America by 1885. The angry Henry Ward Beecher confessed his disillusionment: "We have clubbed them, stoned them, burned their houses, and murdered them," he admitted. With no awareness of inconsistency, he was astonished that these methods had not led to conversions. "I do not know any way, except to blow them up with nitro-glycerine, if we are ever to get them to heaven." [9]

Although Beecher's reference to nitro-glycerin was hyperbolic, other Americans had few scruples about literally using explosives to clear the West of the increasingly undesirable immigrant, thus ending the uncertainty his presence had caused. Peaceful coexistence might have continued had the American economy continued to provide Chinese with noncompetitive opportunities. American businessmen certainly hoped to continue to exploit the Chinese, but their efforts only helped make the Chinese "problem" a national one. For the American worker, the Chinese was coming to have a much more deplorable vice than his failure to become a Christian. In the depressed economy of the 1870s and 1880s, the Chinese became a competitor and a pliable tool of capitalists.

The desire of American businessmen to utilize Chinese in the South and East virtually ensured the Oriental an unfavorable reception in those regions. Two hundred plantation owners met at Memphis in 1869, eager to import Chinese as a lever against former slaves. Stimulated by the enthusiastic rhetoric of Cornelius Koopmanschap, an experienced contractor of Chinese labor, the group resolved to explore the matter. Some Chinese hired on as contract laborers for railroad construction in the South. Others came from Cuba and the Philippines to work the rice and sugar plantations of Mississippi and Louisiana. On the whole, however, the effort was a failure. Koopmanschap himself filed for bankruptcy in 1872. Even more important, the Chinese who had come to the American South left the plantations upon the expiration of their contracts and established small shops. In the long run, the Chinese farm worker proved more costly than the freedmen, since plantation owners were required to pay passage and frequently to provide opium.

Similar developments occurred in the East, where businessmen imported Chinese strikebreakers to destroy nascent labor unions. The owner of a shoe factory in North Adams, Massachusetts, closed by a labor strike in 1870, appears to have been a pioneer. After disappearing for several months, he returned with a Chinese work force. Union organizers greeted the Chinese with the rhetoric of class solidarity. Persuasion failed to deter the Chinese, however, and the strikers were soon working again—at reduced wages and without a union. Learning of the success of the Massachusetts venture, a New Jersey laundry owner secretly brought Chinese in the middle of the night to replace Irish women immigrants. He thus saved himself twenty to thirty dollars a month per worker, as well as further strikes for higher wages. Although sixteen of one hundred women resigned in protest, twelve had begged for reinstatement by the end of the first day the Chinese worked. A mass protest meeting was unsuccessful in undermining the entrepreneur or discouraging the Chinese. The laboring force sulked, but by the end of the year there were three hundred Chinese employed in the laundry.

On the whole, however, the experiments in the East failed as they did in the South, leaving some animosity but no lasting impact. When contracts expired, the Orientals returned to China or to the West Coast, or moved to the more congenial Chinatowns of East Coast cities. Knowing of the hostility among Eastern workers, contractors in California were hesitant to send new Chinese. Meanwhile, with a pool of native workers thrown out of work during the depression of 1873, eastern businessmen had less need to commit themselves to three-year contracts and round-trip tickets.

As a result, only a fraction of the Chinese in nineteenth-century America resided outside the Pacific or Mountain states. As late as 1890, fewer than one in ten Chinese resided elsewhere.

It remained to the West, specifically California with its large concentration of Chinese and long history of Sino-American contact, to perfect control and enclosure and thereby end the confusion and uncertainty generated by the Chinese presence. The negative image that preceded the arrival of Chinese in the Golden State had never been completely eradicated, only subordinated to the need for Chinese labor. Even so, fear of Chinese labor as a threat to free white labor found expression in legislation designed to limit Chinese occupational choices as early as 1850. In that year, the California legislature levied a tax on alien miners. Paid primarily by Chinese, this tax was the major source of revenue for California until the late 1870s.

As the discrimination against Chinese became dominant in the 1870s, California pioneered increasingly restrictive legislation. For example, the state taxed alien fishermen. When Chinese paid the tax and continued to fish, California attempted to deny fishing licenses to aliens. Some measures were obviously discriminatory, such as the higher tax on hand-delivered laundries than on horse-delivered laundries. In 1879, the state constitution banned Chinese from employment by corporations or by the state government. Federal courts eventually declared this provision unconstitutional, but Californians registered their defiance of the national judiciary by refusing to rewrite the voided constitution until after 1900.

When legislative measures were insufficient to control Chinese occupational choices, Californians and other westerners resorted to violence. In 1849, a riot in Chinese Camp, California, inaugurated sixty years of anti-Chinese violence that would drive the Chinese from western mines by 1910. White miners demanded that Chinese not be allowed to hold claims in various cities across California. At Marysville, the resolution was enforced with a marching band and a mob physically escorting Chinese from the California town. Perhaps the peak of Sinophobia occurred in 1885 and 1886, with the massacre of twenty-eight Chinese in Rock Springs, Wyoming, and the forcible expulsion of Chinese from a number of cities along the West Coast, including Seattle and Tacoma. The accidental death of a city councilman in Eureka, California, during a battle between rival Chinese gangs, served as the justification for a mob to demand the hanging of all Chinese in retribution. Frightened that he would be unable to prevent lynchings, the mayor gave the Chinese twenty-four hours to leave the city. A citizens' committee demanded that no Chinese be permitted to return—an unwritten law enforced for more than sixty years. As late as 1937, a newspaper editorial boasted that the county was " 'bad medicine' for the Chinaman." [10] The situation was similar elsewhere in the West. Chinese who arrived to work abandoned Alaskan mines in 1885 were driven out the following year by angry unemployed white and Indian miners armed with dynamite. Arizona and Montana journalists were equally explicit in their condemnation of "the Almond-eyed Mongolian with his pigtail, his heathenism, his filthy habits, his thrift . . . whose tribe we have determined shall not increase in this part of the world." [11]

The declining economic need for unskilled Chinese labor in the interior, plus the growing violence, fostered the enclosure of Chinese in the larger American cities. The chief beneficiary was the Chinatown in San Francisco, long the port of entry into the United States and the home base of most sojourners. The city had never been entirely hospitable to Chinese, whose visibility early attracted Sinophobes. San Franciscans, as early as

1852, described the customs and habits in the negative terms Americans had used in the Celestial Kingdom: "John [Chinaman]'s person does not smell very sweetly; his color and the features of his face are unusual; his penuriousness, his lying, knavery and natural cowardice are proverbial." [12] Prejudice in turn spawned harassment, such as the shearing of a prisoner's queue, the "pigtail" worn by Han Chinese as a symbol of submission to their Manchu conquerors. San Franciscans declared Chinese houses of ill repute a public nuisance in 1866; not until 1874 was the law revised to include fallen women without regard to race, creed, color, or religion. Only Chinese theaters were affected by an ordinance closing public places between one and six in the morning. San Francisco was also headquarters for the California Workingmen's Party, whose slogan was "The Chinese Must Go." The party's issue proved popular enough to become the common property of the state's Democrats and Republicans.

Although San Francisco was scarcely a model of harmony between Chinese and white Americans, it was safer than small towns like Rock Springs, Eureka, Tacoma, or Seattle. Partly as a consequence, the Chinese population of San Francisco increased steadily after 1860. In that year, there were slightly more than 2,700 Chinese in the city, about 8 percent of the state's Chinese residents. The San Francisco census ten years later was 12,000 and 25 percent. The 1880 census counted 21,800 and 29 percent, and by 1890, there were 25,800 Chinese in San Francisco, nearly 36 percent of the state's Chinese. The increasing size of Chinatown was also self-reinforcing. Chinese in small towns throughout the West came to San Francisco to find wives, since they could marry neither whites (thirty-nine states banned miscegenation in the nineteenth century) nor women from their own name clan.

Increasing size changed the function and thus the nature of the Chinatowns. Once a jumping-off point for temporary jobs elsewhere, more and more the Chinatowns became ghettos. Within their confines, the sojourner found a respite from white hostility, resolving the uncertainty he now faced in the United

States. Indeed, a continued stay in the United States required subordination and reduced visibility. The Chinatowns provided both. The Chinese became not merely sojourners but strangers. The culmination of the growing white hostility was exclusion of further Chinese, ending the uncertainty that the Chinese presence caused white Americans. Restricting Chinese immigration meant not only reversing general American policy, but required rewriting treaties with China as well. Mindful of the need for Chinese labor in building the transcontinental railroads promised by the Republican Party, Secretary of State William Henry Seward and Chinese Envoy Anson W. Burlingame had agreed to an unrestricted flow of Chinese to the United States in an 1868 treaty. By then, California had already begun the efforts to impede the flow of Chinese immigrants. As early as 1858 and as late as 1874, the California legislature attempted state legislation to prevent further Chinese immigration. The last of California's efforts was an 1874 law requiring the state commissioner of immigration to ascertain whether incoming passengers who were not citizens might become a public charge or a criminal. If so, the master of the ship had to either post a $500 bond or convey the passenger from California. The Supreme Court declared this statute unconstitutional in 1876, noting that it violated the Burlingame Treaty, the Fourteenth Amendment, and the Civil Rights act of 1874. Unsuccessful in their state efforts, Californians capitalized on their importance in the closely disputed national elections of the Gilded Age to mobilize growing Sinophobia throughout the country and force a renegotiation of the 1868 treaty. In 1880 the Chinese government agreed that the United States could regulate immigration but not "absolutely prohibit it." The Congress promptly decided to deny entry to Chinese laborers for seventy years, a patent evasion of the spirit of the new treaty. When President Rutherford B. Hayes vetoed the bill, Congress reduced the restricted period to ten years. As amended, the bill became law in 1882, denying entrance to skilled as well as unskilled Chinese workers. The measure exempted merchants, students, and travelers, but few fitting these descriptions immigrated to the United States after 1882. The feared Niagara had been dammed to a rivulet.

The Meaning of Chinese Experiences in America

American policies toward the Chinese population, as expressed in the Exclusion Act of 1882 and subsequent amendments, had an impact in three areas: first, in general relations between the United States and China; second, in the development of Chinese communities in the United States; and finally, in regard to other ethnic groups in America.

Discrimination against Chinese in the United States stood in stark contrast to the Open Door treatment the American government was simultaneously demanding from the Chinese. There was, in short, a major contradiction, if not confusion, between the domestic and foreign policies of the United States. At the outset of Western penetration of China, before 1842, Occidental businessmen and missionaries had been confined to the factories at Canton, lest their presence generate friction, as did the Chinese sojourner in the American West. By the end of the nineteenth century, however, Westerners had used warfare and diplomacy to win virtually unrestricted entry into China. Foreign businessmen could reside in more than ninety treaty ports; Western gunboats patrolled coastal waters and the Yangtze River; military units garrisoned several Chinese cities and foreign capitalists gained treaty rights to exploit and develop economic concessions in the interior of China. Beyond the ports, missionaries enjoyed the right to purchase land anywhere. These special privileges foreigners demanded and won in China played a major role in the development of Chinese nationalism.

The confusion in American policies was not lost upon the Chinese. The unequal treatment Chinese experienced in the United States stimulated political self-consciousness in China. Although immigration of coolie labor was prohibited after 1882, American immigration officials continued to harass the exempted classes, so much so that George E. Paulsen has recently described American enforcement of the exclusion acts as "the most important issue" between China and the United States between 1892 and 1904.[13] The discriminatory treatment earned some enmity from the new leadership of China. In 1904 Dr. Sun Yat-sen, the great philosopher and leader of modern Chinese nationalism, was himself detained in a shed near San Francisco for several weeks. Liang Ch'i-ch'ao, a leading Chinese reformer, had been moved to denounce Americans in 1900 as "white bandits" for their treatment of Chinese immigrants.[14] More to the point, in 1905 students and merchants launched a boycott against imports from the United States to protest American policy. The boycott proved an important step for China's revolutions.

The 1882 legislation also had deleterious effects on the Chinese community in the United States, for it froze the population and its unbalanced sexual ratio. By placing Chinese women in the same category as their husbands, most of whom were laborers, the exclusion policy choked the development of Chinese families. Sojourners could not send for their wives. Throughout the nineteenth century, the ratio of men to women among Chinese in America ranged from 18 to 1 to as high as 26 to 1. This suffocation of the Chinese family delayed the appearance of an American-born Chinese community. Under the naturalization laws, Chinese were ineligible for citizenship, though their children were. Bereft of families that might have become absorbed gradually into the larger society, the Chinese community gathered into the Chinatowns of the major cities. Confinement to ghettos heightened the power of the clans; the lack of amenities exacerbated vices such as prostitution and opium-smoking; and exclusion stimulated efforts at illegal entry. Not until World War II and its aftermath on the mainland were American laws relaxed. By 1950, Chinese born in the United States had become a majority of the Chinese community. By 1960, there were 135,000 men and 100,000 Chinese women in America, the most balanced ratio in the history of Chinese in the United States. These recent developments in the Chinese population at last produced a middle class and less identification with the ghetto of Chinatown. The Chinese were thus among the last of the nineteenth-century immigrants to move into American society.

Finally, despite many unique characteristics, the Chinese played a pioneering role in the history of American race and ethnic relations, reflective of the growing uncertainty white Anglo-Saxon Americans were directing toward the "new" immigration. Although the Exclusion Act of 1882 singled out the Chinese as the first immigrant group deemed undesirable as entrants and as citizens, restriction was expanded in the twentieth century. Legal interpretations and an executive agreement between the United States and the Japanese government in 1907 extended exclusion to the Japanese. In the 1920s Congress approached the growing fear of the high social cost of receiving Central and Eastern Europeans as it had the Chinese—by discrimination. The Chinese were also among the first nonwhite, non-Anglo-Saxon Protestants to be forced into the ghetto. Indeed, sociologist Stanford Lyman has emphasized the pivotal importance of the Chinese in the transition of racism from total institutionalization on plantations and reservations to the more subtle, partial, but no less real racism of the twentieth century. The response of white Americans to the Chinese presence, Lyman has written, established the ghetto "as the urban successor to the plantation and the reservation." [15] If his analysis is accurate, then the history of the Sino-American community in the nineteenth century is far more important than sheer numbers would indicate.

Notes

[1] Gunther Barth, *Bitter Strength: A History of the Chinese in the United States, 1850–1870* (Cambridge, Mass., 1964), p. 67.

[2] Quoted in Paul A. Cohen, *China and Christianity: The Missionary Movement and the Growth of Chinese Anti-Foreignism, 1860–1870* (Cambridge, Mass., 1963), p. 85.

[3] Stuart Creighton Miller, "Ends and Means: Missionary Justification of Force in Nineteenth Century China," in *The Missionary Enterprise in China and America,* ed. by John K. Fairbank (Cambridge, Mass., 1974), pp. 249–282. See also Peter W. Fay, "The Protestant Mission and the Opium War," *Pacific Historical Review,* XL (May 1971), 145–161.

[4] Barth, *op. cit.,* p. 44.

[5] Rodman W. Paul, "The Origin of the Chinese Issue in California," *Mississippi Valley Historical Review,* XXV (September 1938), 184. Rose Hum Lee, in *The Chinese in the United States of America* (Hong Kong, 1960), pp. 361–362, cites a 1930s survey of white American beliefs about Chinese. "Their favorite delicacies are rats and snakes" headed the list.

[6] Quoted in Stanford M. Lyman, *The Asian in the West* (Reno and Las Vegas, Nev., 1970), pp. 12–13.

[7] Robert Seager II, "Some Denominational Reactions to Chinese Immigration to California, 1856–1892," *Pacific Historical Review,* XXVIII (February 1959), 50.

[8] Quoted in *ibid.,* p. 51.

[9] Quoted in *ibid.,* p. 60.

[10] Quoted in Lynwood Carranco, "Chinese Expulsion from Humboldt County," *Pacific Historical Review,* XXX (November 1961), 339.

[11] Quoted in Lyman, *op. cit.,* p. 14.

[12] Quoted in *ibid.,* p. 20.

[13] George E. Paulsen, "The Abrogation of the Gresham-Yang Treaty," *Pacific Historical Review,* XL (November 1971), 457.

[14] Harold Z. Schiffrin, *Sun Yat-sen and the Origins of the Chinese Revolution* (Berkeley and Los Angeles, 1970), pp. 186, 327–330.

[15] Lyman, *op. cit.,* p. 8.

Readings and Sources

Barth, Gunther, *Bitter Strength: A History of the Chinese in the United States, 1850–1870* (Cambridge, Mass., 1964). Barth's well-researched work is particularly strong in examining the conditions of Chinese immigration. He argues that the tight organization of the Chinese community contrasted sharply with the plasticity of Californian society, which eventually led to conflict.

Carranco, Lynwood, "Chinese Expulsion from Humboldt County," *Pacific Historical Review,* XXX (November 1961), 329–340. This article centers on the removal of the Chinese from

Eureka in 1885 and the subsequent effort to keep the Chinese from the county.

Carter, Gregg Lee, "Social Demography of the Chinese in Nevada: 1870–1880," *Nevada Historical Society Quarterly,* XVII (Summer 1975), 73–90. Carter's study provides statistical data on the small Chinese community in Nevada. He documents the movement to the urban centers.

Coolidge, Mary R., *Chinese Immigration* (New York, 1909). Coolidge's study, one of the first scholarly treatments of the subject, remains a classic. She emphasizes the importance of California in the movement to restrict Chinese.

Fay, Peter W., "The Protestant Mission and the Opium War," *Pacific Historical Review,* XL (May 1971), 145–161. Fay argues that both British and American missionaries in China were hostile to the Chinese and viewed the Opium War as a welcome opportunity to open China to Christianity.

Lee, Rose Hum, *The Chinese in the United States of America* (Hong Kong, 1960). Lee, a sociologist, has gathered much data, with a strong emphasis on the contemporary assimilation of Chinese in the United States. She views assimilation as both desirable and essential.

Lin, Han-sheng, "Chinese Immigrants in the United States: Achievements and Problems," *Peace and Change,* III (Summer-Fall 1975), 52–67. Lin believes that the traditional Chinese indifference to political participation ill-served Chinese-Americans in the past. He emphasizes the achievements of Chinese-Americans since the repeal of immigration restriction and the acquisition of citizenship. He also urges the newer immigrants and the younger generation of Chinese to work together to solve remaining problems, especially those that confront older Chinese still residing in the Chinatowns.

Liu, Kwang-Ching, "America and China: The Late Nineteenth Century," *American-East Asian Relations: A Survey,* edited by Ernest R. May and James C. Thomson, Jr. (Cambridge, Mass., 1972). Liu surveys the current literature and maps out new areas for further exploration.

Lyman, Stanford M., *The Asian in the West* (Reno and Las Vegas, Nev., 1970). In this collection of essays, Lyman builds a strong case for the importance of the Chinese-American community in what he described as the partially institutionalized racism of contemporary America. His historical framework is sound and persuasive.

————, *Chinese-Americans* (New York, 1974). This is probably the best single work on the Chinese in the United States.

McClellan, Robert, *Heathen Chinee: A Study of American Attitudes toward China, 1890–1905* (Columbus, Ohio, 1970). McClellan's work deals primarily with the attitudes Americans held of Chinese in the United States.

Miller, Stuart Creighton, "Ends and Means: Missionary Justification of Force in Nineteenth Century China," in *The Missionary Enterprise in China and America,* edited by John K. Fairbank (Cambridge, Mass., 1974). Miller's account of the sanguinary relationship between missionaries and Chinese is devasting.

————, *The Unwelcome Immigrant: The American Image of the Chinese, 1785–1882* (Berkeley and Los Angeles, 1969). Miller explains the hostile reception of Chinese in the United States through an examination of reports from China hands. He emphasizes negative images.

Paul, Rodman W., "The Origin of the Chinese Issue in California," *Mississippi Valley Historical Review,* XXV (September 1938), 191–196. Paul argues that the hostility developed among white miners toward all foreigners was transferred to the Chinese, who as early as the 1850s were already the target for political attacks and racial discrimination.

Paulsen, George E., "The Abrogation of the Gresham-Yang Treaty," *Pacific Historical Review,* XL (November 1971), 457–477. Paulsen points out that the Chinese government considered the narrow interpretations the customs officials gave to enforcement of the exclusion acts "the most important issue with the United States" at the turn of the century.

Sandmeyer, Elmer Clarence, *The Anti-Chinese Movement in California* (Champaign, Ill., 1939). Sandmeyer views the origin of California restrictions on the Chinese in both racial antagonism and economic competition. When efforts to secure relief through local and state legislation failed, Californians used their political leverage to force federal legislation.

Saxton, Alexander, "The Army of Canton in the High Sierra," *Pacific Historical Review,* XXXV (May 1966), 141–152. The Chinese provided almost 90 percent of the work force for the building of the Central Pacific. Saxton views their role as indispensable.

————, *The Indispensable Enemy: Labor and the Anti-Chinese Movement in California* (Berkeley and Los Angeles, 1971). While Saxton's account focuses on the importance of anti-Chinese sentiment to labor in California, he finds the roots of that sentiment in Jacksonian ideology. Hostility toward the Chinese was, in his view, national rather than peculiar to California or the West Coast.

Seager, Robert, II, "Some Denominational Reactions to Chinese

Immigration to California, 1856–1892," *Pacific Historical Review,* XXVIII (February 1959), 49–66. Seager points out that the missionaries provided one force for the amelioration of the harsh response to Chinese in the United States. As he notes, however, by the 1880s the prominent missionaries to the Chinese community in the United States were willing to cast their lot with restriction.

Sung, Betty Lee, *Mountain of Gold: The Story of the Chinese in America* (New York, 1967). A popular account of the Chinese experience, Sung's anecdotal approach stresses the movement of the Chinese into the American middle class.

Weiss, Melford S., *Valley City: A Chinese Community in America* (Cambridge, Mass., 1974). Weiss, a sociologist, has made an in-depth study of the Chinese community in a central California city.

Chapter Three

The Open Door and Integrity of China, 1899-1922: Hazy Principles for Changing Policy

BY RAYMOND A. ESTHUS

In the first four decades of the twentieth century, the principles of the open door and the integrity of China gave to American Far Eastern policy an appearance of consistency. In actuality this was an illusion, for change and confusion, rather than
uniformity, characterized American policy. The principles were
subjected to varying and hazy definitions; American leaders
were often unsure about what the principles meant or should
mean; and as a result, leaders and diplomats of other nations
experienced bewilderment in attempting to understand the
American principles and their application in American foreign
policy.

About one aspect of the principles there was no doubt: their
origin. It was the descent of the powers on China in the 1890s
that impelled John Hay to issue his famous turn-of-the-century
pronouncements on the open door and the integrity of China.
A. E. Hippisley, of the Chinese customs service, and W. W.
Rockhill, Hay's adviser, who together drafted the open door
notes of September 6, 1899, were keenly aware that equal
trading opportunities and indeed China's existence as a nation
were imperiled by the concessions exacted from the hapless
Middle Kingdom. In the single year 1898 Germany, Russia,
France, and Britain secured leases on navy base sites on the

China coast. Even more significant, through railway concessions and other grants in the years from 1895 to 1898, those powers marked out spheres of influence in China—areas that Hippisley appropriately described as "the economic and geographical gravitation of certain portions of the Chinese Empire." [1]

A Limited Commitment and an Uncertain Policy

The confusion over the open door policy began with the open door notes themselves. The notes did not ask for the abolition of the spheres. They asked only that within the spheres there be no interference with treaty ports and tariffs and no discriminatory railway rates or harbor dues. The issue of preferential or exclusive investment rights enjoyed by sphere-holding powers was not addressed. The notes did not, however, recognize the spheres. The communication sent to London even stated explicitly that the United States would "in no way commit itself to a recognition of exclusive rights of any power within or control over any portion of the Chinese Empire." The withholding of recognition of the spheres, coupled with the request for equal trading rights *within* the spheres, caused confusion in foreign capitals. The manner in which Hay handled the replies of the powers caused further puzzlement, at least in St. Petersburg. The governments that sent affirmative replies made their agreement contingent on everyone's assent, and the Russian reply fell far short of being responsive to the American note. The Russian government agreed only to refrain from interfering with China's collection of customs duties, and it ignored the other American requests. Hay blandly pretended that the reply was favorable. "We got all that could be screwed out of the Bear," he wrote to Henry Adams, "and our cue is to insist we got everything." [2] Russia, of course, knew—and the other powers probably suspected—that Hay had not gotten everything; but this did not dissuade the resourceful Secretary of State from declaring in March 1900 that the replies were satisfactory and indeed were "final and definitive."

Whatever the confusions and ambiguities surrounding the open door notes, Hay's next pronouncement raised new problems by accentuating a fundamental contradiction in American policy. On July 3, 1900, in the midst of the Boxer uprising, Hay sent a circular to the powers calling for a settlement of the Boxer troubles that would preserve Chinese territorial and administrative entity. For the next four decades the integrity of China principle would occupy a prominent place in the rhetoric of United States policy. But how could this principle be reconciled with the spheres of influence, which the notes of September 1899 had tacitly accepted? The spheres of influence obviously infringed China's integrity.

Some compromise had to be found between the conflicting elements of American policy. A possible middle ground was to tolerate existing special rights but oppose acquisitions of additional rights. Only Germany in its Shantung sphere possessed an exclusive investment monopoly. The treaties secured by Russia, France, and Britain fell short of granting exclusive spheres. The claims of those nations to spheres rested only on specific railway and mining concessions and in the cases of France and Britain on agreements pledging China not to alienate territory in their spheres. The United States was thus free to resist further development of the spheres and thereby defend what remained of United States rights and China's integrity.

The American commitment to the integrity of China principle was, in any case, limited—so limited that the McKinley administration did not hesitate to join in the scramble for navy bases. In November 1900 the American minister at Peking was instructed to broach the possibility of a United States Navy base at Samsah Bay on the coast of Fukien. The matter was soon dropped, but not before Hay suffered the embarrassment of being reminded by Japan of the recent American statement in support of China's integrity.[3]

When Russia refused to withdraw troops from Manchuria following the Boxer uprising, the United States again showed scant concern for the principle of China's integrity. Washington limited its efforts to preserving the open door for commerce and resisting Russia's acquisition of new economic rights. In February 1902 Hay, now Secretary of State in the new Roosevelt administration, protested Russia's demands for exclusive railway, mining, and industrial rights in Manchuria, although he betrayed no concurrent alarm over the threat of Russian political control. In a letter to Roosevelt, Hay succinctly expressed the policy of the administration:

> We are not in any attitude of hostility towards Russia in Manchuria. On the contrary, we recognize her exceptional position in northern China. What we have been working for two years to accomplish . . . is that no matter what happens eventually in northern China and Manchuria, the United States shall not be placed in any worse position than while the country was under the unquestioned domination of China.[4]

The Japanese attack on Russia in February 1904 and the ensuing Japanese victories enabled Roosevelt and Hay to restore to American policy the concept of China's integrity, including Chinese sovereignty over Manchuria. Since, however, the war was destined to be fought largely in Manchuria, the implementation of the principle had to be restricted. The result was new confusion over American policy. Hay appealed to the belligerents in February 1904 "to respect the neutrality of China and in all practicable ways her administrative entity," but he did not make clear how his admonition applied to Manchuria. The British government in particular was puzzled by the fact that Hay drew no boundary between the war area and the neutral area. Hay sent a clarification to London, but it did not clarify. "The proposal of this government," he explained, "does not contemplate definition of neutral limits but aims to secure the smallest possible area of hostilities and the largest possible area of neutrality compatible with the military necessities of the two belligerents in their hostile operations against each other." When London sought further clarification, Hay recorded in his diary that the British seemed "very dull in taking the fact that it is unnecessary to state in a note like this the notorious fact that there is war in Manchuria and in Korea." [5]

The British were again puzzled when in January 1905 Hay undertook another diplomatic initiative. This time Hay reaffirmed the principles of the open door and the integrity of China and urged the neutral powers not to seek territorial concessions in China when the war ended. What confused the British was that in that same month President Roosevelt told the British Ambassador that the United States would not seriously oppose Russian annexation of northern Manchuria. This statement came as part of an endeavor by Roosevelt to bring British and American policy into accord, so British leaders rightly regarded it as more than a casual statement. In a letter to Foreign Secretary Lansdowne, Prime Minister Arthur Balfour questioned how Britain could pledge respect for the integrity of China and at the same time agree to Russian acquisition of northern Manchuria. Without entirely resolving their puzzlement, the British told Roosevelt that they would not object to Russia having a direct railway line to Vladivostok through territory under its own control. The British were also confused about the geography of the area. In a note to Balfour, Lansdowne referred to giving the Russians a "corner" of Manchuria. A glance at a map would have shown him that the area enclosing the Chinese Eastern Railway constituted half of Manchuria.[6]

With the death of John Hay in the summer of 1905, the implementation of the hazy principles of the open door and the integrity of China was left to Roosevelt and his new Secretary of State, Elihu Root. Manchuria continued to be the principal arena for the testing of those principles, but the conclusion of peace between Russia and Japan in September 1905 created a new context for their application. By the Portsmouth Peace Treaty the Russian navy base at Port Arthur and most of the trunk railway line running to it went to Japan. Russia retained its rights in northern Manchuria but without any acquisition of territory. Roosevelt and Root thus had to deal with two spheres of influence in Manchuria, a Russian sphere in the north and a

Japanese sphere in the south. By the peace treaty Manchuria was at least nominally restored to China, but the Russians and the Japanese held such extensive rights there that China's sovereignty in the area remained seriously impaired. This was especially true in the south where the Japanese railway, known as the South Manchuria Railway (SMR), became the base for many Japanese enterprises.

In the postwar years Roosevelt displayed little concern about the open door and the integrity of China as applied to Manchuria. This resulted from the fact that he had great respect for Japan's strategic position in Manchuria. If the Japanese in the course of defending strategic interests in south Manchuria infringed the rights of other nations, Roosevelt was not inclined to take them to task.

Roosevelt's attitude regarding Japan's position in Manchuria was evident on many occasions. After Japan's initial victories in the Russo-Japanese War, he told Minister Takahira Kogorō and special envoy Kaneko Kentarō that he personally believed that Japan should have a "paramount interest" in what surrounded the Yellow Sea. Following the battle of Mukden in 1905, he told Takahira that Japan had gained "dominance" in Manchuria. During the Portsmouth Peace Conference, he told the Japanese that they had won "control" of Manchuria. In 1908 he told Takahira that in matters relating to China's sovereignty, he was willing to treat Manchuria differently from the rest of China. Two years later in a letter to his successor, President Taft, Roosevelt gave the most revealing insight into his attitude. He said that Japan's powers, interests, and intentions in Manchuria must be judged "on the actual facts of the case, and not by mere study of treaties." [7]

Unknown to Roosevelt, one of his own diplomats held views directly opposite to his and even undertook an anti-Japanese crusade in Manchuria. During the years 1906–1908 the American Consul General at Mukden, Willard Straight, sought to redefine the open door policy to include equal investment opportunity. His aim was no less than to destroy the Japanese sphere of influence by injecting into Manchuria the superior capital resources of the United States. He first tried to organize a Manchurian Bank through which he hoped American capital could dominate investment enterprise in Manchuria. When uncertain financial conditions on Wall Street frustrated this scheme, he turned his attention to a railway project being devised by his British friends J. O. P. Bland and Lord ffrench. This was an undertaking to construct a railway line from Hsinmintun to Fakumen and eventually to Tsitsihar paralleling Japan's South Manchuria Railway. In a candid letter to F. M. Huntington Wilson, the Third Assistant Secretary of State, Straight admitted that the railway line was designed to compete seriously with the SMR and that it would even threaten the Japanese strategic position in Manchuria. Lack of British diplomatic support, together with Japanese objections, eventually killed the project, but by that time Straight was working on a new scheme to check the Japanese. The United States was at this time negotiating the return to China of a portion of the Boxer indemnity payments, and Straight sought to get these funds for his Manchurian development program. Straight was again blocked, however, this time by Rockhill, who was now Minister at Peking. Rockhill had no sympathy for Straight's activities, and he convinced Roosevelt and Root that the funds should go to educate Chinese students in the United States.[8]

Straight's experiences showed that neither Washington nor Wall Street had any great interest in pushing American interests in Manchuria. Straight could not even arouse merchants about ordinary trading opportunities in Manchuria. Published consular reports relayed his pleas for more energetic American commercial efforts, but no one heeded. "When all is said and done," Straight wrote to William Phillips, "it's a rather thankless task, this endeavor to increase the American export trade. Our merchants, at least those who have addressed inquiries to this office, are not prepared to expend either time or trouble introducing their wares abroad." [9]

As for the Japanese, they were both irritated and confused by Straight's activities. Japanese leaders knew of Roosevelt's oft-expressed friendship for Japan and his beneficent attitude toward their interests on the Asian continent. They were therefore puzzled by Straight's anti-Japanese program and by his new definition of the open door policy.

The definition of the open door that ultimately prevailed during the Roosevelt administration was fashioned neither by Straight nor by Roosevelt. The Secretary of State, Elihu Root, made the strongest imprint on policy. Root's views fell somewhere between Roosevelt's beneficence and Straight's hostility toward Japan. Unlike Roosevelt, who believed Japan's interests in Manchuria should be judged by the actual facts rather than by "mere study of treaties," Root believed that the rights of Japan were no more than the sum of its treaty rights. Furthermore, in interpreting those treaty rights Root gave great weight to China's integrity. Root did not believe like Straight, however, that Japan's legally established rights should be subjected to attack.

Root's evenhanded attitude was evident in 1907–1908 when Russia attempted to assert administrative rights over Harbin, claiming that this Chinese city was part of the zone of the Chinese Eastern Railway. Root knew that if Russia could make good its claim, Japan could assert the same right along the route of the South Manchuria Railway. William Phillips, head of the department's new Division of Far Eastern Affairs, advised Root that in such an eventuality, "The integrity of China would be at an end." [10] Root took the initiative in urging other governments to resist the Russian claim and in urging Japan not to advance a similar claim. He was reluctant to become a protagonist for China, but he thought that the Russian claim had to be opposed. Phillips, in a letter to Rockhill, accurately described Root's attitude:

I do not think that the Department intends to have trouble in Manchuria, either with Russia or Japan. The Secretary is especially anxious not to become embroiled in little incidents with either of those two powers; but when Russia makes a demand that we relinquish our extraterritorial rights in Harbin and on all railway property, in favor of Russia, we can not very well agree to her proposal without hitting China pretty hard. [11]

The Japanese knew from Root's attitude on the Harbin question that he would not accord them a free hand in Manchuria. Renewed confirmation of this came in the negotiations leading to the Root-Takahira exchange of notes in November 1908. These negotiations were undertaken primarily to achieve an entente that would still the war rumors generated by the Japanese immigration question. Such a project, however, could not ignore the issues of the open door and the integrity of China. At the outset of the negotiations, Japan was willing to reaffirm support for the open door but preferred to leave out any declaration concerning China's integrity. Root agreed to omit direct consideration of the Harbin question, thus postponing that debate, but he insisted on a clause supporting China's integrity. In formulating that provision he acquiesced in the deletion of any mention of China's "administrative entity," perhaps because it would impinge too much on the Harbin question, but he successfully insisted on including a statement supporting China's "independence and integrity." Other clauses supporting the status quo and the open door were in line with Root's middle-of-the-road policy.[12] Support of the status quo meant, in a sense, recognition of Japan's treaty rights in China, but it did not mean Japan was free further to violate China's integrity by securing more rights or by making unreasonable interpretations of existing rights. What the exchange of notes meant for the open door was less clear. The notes clearly reaffirmed support for equal opportunity for commerce, but the question of investment rights remained vague. Japan had never specifically asserted a claim to *exclusive* investment rights in its sphere, and the United States had never recognized Japan's possession of any such rights. To what extent the United States would accord Japan a *preferential* status for capital investment in Manchuria remained unclear.

Insofar as the Roosevelt administration crystallized an official policy on the open door and the integrity of China, it came in the course of the Harbin dispute and the Root-Takahira negotiations. The policy reflected the legalistic views of Root rather than the *Realpolitik* of Roosevelt. It would be a mistake, however, to draw too great a distinction between the attitudes of Root and Roosevelt. They shared the fundamental view that every effort should be made to make advocacy of the open door and integrity of China compatible with friendship with Japan. If they had felt compelled to choose between Japan's friendship and China's interests, there is little doubt that they would have opted for Japan. The principles of the open door and the integrity of China, by whatever definition, were not foreign policy objectives to be pursued with unlimited resolve and commitment.

Taft Chooses China

When the Taft administration took office in March 1909, it quickly scrapped the moderate policy of Roosevelt and Root in favor of Straight's anti-Japanese crusade. The State Department inspired the formation of an American banking group to exploit investment opportunities in China. The new financial combination, composed of J. P. Morgan and Company, Kuhn, Loeb and Company, the National City Bank, and the First National Bank, named Straight its chief overseas agent. At the State Department Huntington Wilson, who shared Straight's views about Japan, became First Assistant Secretary of State. President Taft and the new Secretary of State, Philander C. Knox, enthusiastically accepted the definition of the open door that these activists had long championed, a policy that demanded equal investment rights as well as equal commercial rights. This policy of dollar diplomacy sought to stimulate the flow of American capital into China and to increase American influence at Peking.

Although Manchuria was to be the principal arena of dollar diplomacy in China, in its first months the new administration focused its attention on China south of the Great Wall. There the spheres of influence were softening. In May 1909 Britain, France, and Germany agreed to cooperate on construction of a railway running from Canton to Hankow and then west to Chungtu. To this project, known as the Hukuang railway, the Taft administration immediately demanded admission of American financial interests. The Department of State even threatened to reconsider the remission of the Boxer indemnity funds if China did not agree to American participation. The matter dragged on for a year, but finally in May 1910 China agreed to admit the American bankers to the project. Six months later the banking groups of Britain, France, Germany, and the United States formed a four-power consortium and agreed to share equally in Chinese railway loans.

In the meantime, Straight had revived his campaign against the Japanese in Manchuria with a project that resembled the ill-fated Hsinmintun-Fakumen railway scheme. In October 1909 he secured a preliminary agreement with the Manchurian Governor-General, Hsi-liang, for the construction of a railway from Chinchow to Aigun. The American banking group was to provide financing, and the British firm Pauling and Company was to handle construction. The line was farther to the west than the Hsin-Fa project, but since it was designed to link up with Russia's Chinese Eastern Railway, it threatened Japan's South Manchuria Railway. The Chinese recognized the political character of the undertaking. Hsi-liang told his superiors in Peking that if Manchuria were to be saved from Japan, the strength of both the United States and Britain must be brought in to counter the Japanese. Though the Chin-Ai project was called a commercial railway, said Hsi-liang, it was in fact "part of a diplomatic and political policy." [13]

Before the Japanese reacted to the Chin-Ai project, Knox unveiled an even more breathtaking scheme. In November he proposed to London that the United States and Britain sponsor a project to neutralize the railways in Manchuria. Under the plan the powers would lend China the money to purchase the railways from Russia and Japan, and the lines would be under international control during the period of the loan. Knox proposed that if neutralization proved impracticable, then Britain and the United States should go forward with the Chin-Ai project, inviting participation of powers friendly to the com-

plete commercial neutralization of Manchuria. With only equivo-
cal support from London, Knox sprang the proposals on the
other powers. The upshot was categorical rejection of the neutralization scheme by both Japan and Russia. The Chin-Ai project was not so firmly rebuffed, but in subsequent negotiations
it also collapsed.

The bewilderment these events caused in foreign capitals was
not due—as in the Roosevelt period—to confusion over the
definition given to the principles of the open door and the
integrity of China. The definition was all too clear. The con-
sternation was due rather to the great gap in American policy
between means and objectives. The British Minister at Peking,
Sir John Jordan, described Knox's proposals as "a scheme so
vast and fantastic as almost to stagger the imagination." Knox
somehow assumed that the Japanese would meekly bow to his
proposals. Far from being in a mood to bow, the Japanese,
according to British Ambassador Claude MacDonald, had been
"electrified" by the neutralization proposal. MacDonald's assessment was doubtless correct. On receiving the American proposals, Foreign Minister Komura Jutarō had exclaimed: "They
are asking us to internationalize what is our own property, acquired by us at the cost of much treasure and many lives." [14]

The abortive Knox proposals gave a new impetus to efforts
by Russia and Japan to achieve closer cooperation. Shortly
before the neutralization scheme was proposed in November
1909, Japan had sounded out Russia on the possibilities of a
treaty that would go beyond an entente concluded in 1907.
Then in April 1910 in the wake of the Knox proposals, Russo-
Japanese negotiations began. On July 4 two treaties were concluded, one public and one secret. The public agreement, unlike the entente of 1907, refrained from mentioning the open
door and the integrity of China. Russia and Japan engaged to
lend each other friendly cooperation in improving their railway lines in Manchuria. The two powers also declared support
for the status quo. The provisions of the secret accord indicated that the term status quo meant their special positions
in Manchuria. Indeed, status quo was interpreted to encom-

pass expansion of their special rights. The secret treaty obligated the signatories not to hinder the "consolidation and further development" of each other's special rights. The agreement even pledged the two powers to common action in defense of their special interests. Sir Edward Grey, who knew of the secret as well as the public agreement, believed that United States policy had helped to produce the Russo-Japanese entente. He wrote Ambassador James Bryce at Washington that the only apparent result of Knox's proposals had been to draw Russia and Japan closer together and to make the task of preserving the open door more difficult.[15]

As Knox stood amidst the wreckage of his policy, his own banking group lost confidence in his leadership. At a meeting in September 1910, the bankers told him bluntly that they were not interested in serving as the instrument of an aggressive policy in China and that they would continue as the State Department's financial agent only if they were not asked to undertake projects that aroused the unbending opposition of the powers.[16]

Dollar diplomacy in China was based at least in part on laudable objectives—the broadening of the open door concept and the support of China's integrity—but the policy was so poorly thought through and so hastily and clumsily implemented that it was completely counterproductive. Knox and his associates approached power realities with incredible naïveté. However worthy the policy objectives, successful China policy could have been achieved only by skillful manipulation of the relationships between the powers. It is possible that no amount of diplomatic skill could have reversed the march of events in Manchuria, where Russian and Japanese imperialism appeared to be propelled by inexorable forces, but a more skillful execution of American policy at least might have wrought less havoc. As it was, the United States greatly contributed to hardening the Manchurian spheres. Ironically, with all his energetic activity, Knox did not alter the apathy of American commercial interests. William J. Calhoun, the American Minister at Peking, reported in 1912 that Americans were not interested in pushing the China trade. Calhoun asked Knox what difference it made whether the door was open or shut "if we are not disposed to go in or out of it, even when it is open?" [17]

Restraining Japan with Concessions

When the Wilson administration took office in 1913, policy choices were considerably more circumscribed than they had been four years earlier for Taft. In Manchuria the Japanese and Russians had dug in. Other developments in East Asia were also making defense of the open door and the integrity of China increasingly difficult. The overthrow of the Ch'ing dynasty in 1912 inaugurated political turmoil in China. Two years later the outbreak of war in Europe greatly weakened the European presence in China and left the United States and Japan as the principal rivals. In this context the Wilson administration never considered policy of the Knox-Straight variety. Rather it adopted a defensive policy and fought a rearguard action as it fell back from one position to another. In retreat, the Wilson administration was to suffer defeats even more serious than those inflicted on the preceding administration.

Failures in America's China policy during the years 1913–1920 were not due entirely to Far Eastern developments: The setbacks came in part from confusions within the administration. President Wilson, Secretary of State William Jennings Bryan, and the State Department Counselor, Robert Lansing, who was to succeed Bryan in 1915, had great difficulty sorting out objectives and developing means to attain them. One source of confusion was the differing attitudes of Wilson and Lansing. Wilson had a strong interest in China's integrity; Lansing was primarily interested in the open door. Lansing was willing to trade concessions on China's integrity to protect commercial rights, or even to quiet Japanese complaints about mistreatment of Japanese aliens in California.

The low priority Lansing gave to the integrity of China was evident when at the outbreak of World War I in 1914 China vainly sought United States help in restraining Japan from seizing the German sphere in Shantung. As Acting Secretary of State on that occasion, he informed the United States chargé at Peking that though the United States desired China to feel that American friendship was sincere, "it would be quixotic in the extreme to allow the question of China's territorial integrity to entangle the United States in international difficulties." [18]

Capitalizing on the opportunities presented by the World War, Japan proceeded to seize German rights and interests in Shantung. Then in January 1915 Tokyo presented to Peking the notorious Twenty-one Demands. These demands, divided into five groups, constituted the most blatant imperialism Japan had ever practiced in its relations with China. The first four groups demanded China's assent to the transference of German rights in Shantung, vast new rights in south Manchuria and eastern Inner Mongolia, certain mining rights in the Yangtze Valley, and a commitment by China not to lease or cede any territory on its coast. The demands of Group V, which the Japanese insisted were only "wishes" or "requests," were even more sweeping. This group proposed acceptance by China of Japanese political, military, and financial advisers, establishment of Sino-Japanese police forces in certain areas of China, preference for Japan in arms sales to China, and recognition of Fukien as a Japanese sphere of influence.

Once the demands were fully known in Washington, Wilson, Bryan, and Lansing agreed that the United States should seek to restrain Japan, but they were uncertain about how this could be done. Bryan and Lansing were inclined to let the Japanese have their way in northern China and to concentrate United States efforts on opposing Group V. Lansing proposed that the United States admit that Japan had "special interests" in Manchuria and Inner Mongolia in the hope that Japan would reciprocate by observing restraint in the rest of China and by ceasing complaints over mistreatment of Japanese in California.

Bryan was willing to compromise China's integrity even further. "I am not sure," he wrote to Wilson, "but that it would be worth while for China to agree to the cession of Manchuria to Japan if, by doing so, she could secure freedom as to the rest of the country." [19]

The first important American pronouncement came on March 13, 1915, in a protest to Japan. Drafted by Lansing and E. T. Williams, chief of the Far Eastern Division, the communication objected to Group V of the Twenty-one Demands on the grounds that these requests "would exclude Americans from equal participation in the economic and industrial development of China and would limit the political independence of that country." The note went on to give an extraordinary recognition of Japan's special position in specific areas of China. In discussing the demands of Group I and Group II, relating to Shantung, south Manchuria, and eastern Inner Mongolia, the note said that although the United States had grounds for objections under its treaties with China, it would not protest "at this time" because it "frankly recognizes that territorial contiguity creates special relations between Japan and these districts." [20]

Formal recognition of special relations based on territorial contiguity was an unprecedented concession to the Japanese. In 1904 Theodore Roosevelt had told the Japanese that they should have a paramount interest in the area surrounding the Yellow Sea, but he had cautioned the Japanese that this was only his private view. Such a theory had never been set down in an official diplomatic note to Tokyo. Lansing, Bryan, and Wilson soon regretted that they had made such a sweeping concession—they even tried to convince themselves that there had been no concession—but the deed was done. Not even the qualification "at this time" could provide an avenue of escape. That phrase obviously applied to whether or not the United States might protest specific demands. It could not put a time limit on the general principle of special relations based on territorial contiguity.

Bryan compounded the blunder by proposing compromises

for Group V. He suggested to Japan that China be required to agree not to discriminate against the Japanese in the appointment of advisers and in the purchase of arms and that Japanese police be employed only in Manchuria and eastern Inner Mongolia. This stunned the United States Minister at Peking, Paul Reinsch. He telegraphed Bryan that if China knew the United States favored proposals wherein China would forgo its freedom to choose advisers whom it trusted, to buy arms as it pleased, and to exercise police functions in territory under its sovereignty, Chinese leaders would conclude that the United States had betrayed its friendship for China and its moral responsibility in respect to the principles of China's integrity and the open door. Reinsch told Bryan bluntly that it would be better for the United States to stay out of the controversy than to give China that kind of help. Through some strange process of rationalization, Wilson and Bryan soon convinced themselves that China had not been betrayed, either by Bryan's compromise proposals or by the March 13 note. Wilson told Bryan to inform Reinsch that the United States had not acquiesced in *any* of Japan's demands. Bryan thereupon telegraphed Reinsch that the United States had not acquiesced in anything that violated China's rights or disregarded the interests of the United States.[21]

The rationalization was carried another step. As the Sino-Japanese negotiations on the Twenty-one Demands approached a climax in May 1915, the Wilson administration convinced itself that it could wipe the slate clean. On May 10 Wilson wrote to Bryan: "It will not do to leave any of our rights indefinite or to seem to acquiesce in any part of the Japanese plan which violates the solemn understanding of the nations with regard to China." [22] The following day Bryan sent to Japan and China his famous nonrecognition notes. Like the March 13 note, the new statement of policy was largely the handiwork of Lansing. It stated that the United States could not recognize

> any agreement or undertaking which has been entered into or which may be entered into between the Governments of Japan and China, impairing the treaty rights of the United

States and its citizens in China, the political or territorial integrity of the Republic of China, or the international policy relative to China commonly known as the open door policy.[23]

Just how Wilson, Bryan, and Lansing reconciled this position with the March 13 note is not clear, nor was it clear to the Japanese.

However much the Japanese may have been confused by American diplomacy, they had no grounds for confusion about the attitude of their allies the British. As early as February 1915 Sir Edward Grey had urged the Japanese not to advance demands impairing the integrity or independence of China. Such demands, he said, could not be reconciled with the terms of the Anglo-Japanese Alliance.[24] The London government stuck to this position, and doubtless this influence caused Japan to moderate its position in the negotiations. Though in the agreements concluded in May 1915 Japan obtained most of what it demanded, particularly regarding Shantung and south Manchuria, the Tokyo government agreed to "postpone" most of the proposals in Group V.

The confusion over China policy evident during the crisis over the Twenty-one Demands unfortunately did not disappear. Another muddle occurred early in 1917. In January of that year, Reinsch suggested to the Japanese Minister at Peking that the United States and Japan undertake joint ventures in railway construction in south Manchuria. The Japanese government, startled by this proposal, made inquiries at Washington. Lansing, now Secretary of State, assured Japanese Ambassador Sato Aimaro that the American government recognized Japan's special interests in Manchuria and that the United States did not wish to interfere with Japan's interests there. Lansing said that south Manchuria was in a different category than Shantung, where the United States had recognized no such special status. Lansing obviously had forgotten that the note of March 13, 1915, had recognized Japan's special relationship with south Manchuria, eastern Inner Mongolia, and Shantung. Wilson apparently could not keep track of what had been recognized either, for when he read a report of Lansing's talk with Sato, he wrote to Lansing that he had taken the right position throughout the conversation.[25]

The entrance of the United States into World War I in the spring of 1917 turned circumstances even more in favor of Japan. Like the European powers, the United States had to give principal attention to the war. Japan did not refrain from pressing its advantage. In the summer of 1917, it dispatched a special mission to the United States headed by Ishii Kikujirō, ostensibly to bring cooperation in the war effort, but more importantly to secure clarification of Wilson's China policy. Wilson and Lansing welcomed the mission, hoping to get from the Tokyo government a reaffirmation of the open door and the integrity of China.

The Lansing-Ishii negotiations, which got under way in September 1917, confirmed the continuing contradictions of American policy toward China. At the outset the Japanese made it clear that they would pledge support for those principles only in return for recognition of their special interests in China. Lansing and Wilson were willing to meet this paradoxical condition. Lansing framed a clause stating that the two nations "recognize that territorial propinquity creates special relations between countries; and consequently the Government of the United States recognizes that Japan has special interests in China, particularly in the part to which her possessions are contiguous." This recognition went beyond the note of March 13, 1915, which had recognized Japan's special relationship only with specific districts of China, namely south Manchuria, eastern Inner Mongolia, and Shantung. Lansing now agreed to recognize Japan's special interests *in China,* particularly—but not exclusively—in the part contiguous to her possessions. In return for this sweeping concession, Lansing sought two things: (1) an unequivocal reaffirmation of support for the open door and the integrity of China, and (2) a pledge that the two parties would not "take advantage of present conditions to seek special rights or privileges in China which would abridge the rights of the citizens or subjects of other friendly states." [26]

The Japanese were willing to reaffirm the open door and the

integrity of China, but balked at the pledge of good behavior. Lansing and Ishii then worked out a compromise. Recognition of Japan's special interests in China and reaffirmation of the American principles would be proclaimed in a public exchange of notes; the pledge not to take advantage of conditions in China would be relegated to a secret protocol. Wilson and the Tokyo government approved this arrangement, and the two agreements were concluded on November 2, 1917. The secret protocol was worded in such a way, however, that it was uncertain whether it bound Japan to anything. It quoted the clause proposed by Lansing, but went on to say that the clause was "superfluous" and had been eliminated from the declaration. The document then asserted that the principle enunciated in the suppressed clause was in "perfect accord with the declared policy of the two Governments in regard to China." [27] The protocol thus declared the fact of an existing policy. It was questionable whether the protocol could be interpreted as binding for future policy.

By the end of the war, the Wilson administration had little evidence of success in its attempt to restrain Japan through concessions, and the Paris Peace Conference in 1919 brought Wilson and Lansing no closer to their elusive goal. On the contrary, the peace conference brought into sharp focus the self-defeating nature of the concession policy. The Japanese delegates came to the conference resolved to gain formal sanction for acquisition of the German rights in Shantung, and they came armed with a fistful of treaties and diplomatic notes: China's assent given to the transfer of rights in 1915, and given again by another treaty in 1918; secret treaties with Britain, France, and Russia pledging support for the Japanese claim; the United States note of March 13, 1915; and finally the Lansing-Ishii exchange of notes. The United States, through its recognition of Japan's special interests in 1915 and 1917, had made a significant contribution to Japan's legal and moral position at the peace conference. It is not surprising that Wilson, along with the others of the Big Four, gave in to the Japanese demand at Paris. What is surprising is that Lansing, who had played a major role in the recognition of Japan's special interests, had the temerity to criticize Wilson's decision. But criticize it he did, both within the American delegation at Paris and later in testimony before the Senate Foreign Relations Committee.

Rebuilding the Open Door and the Integrity of China Policy

It was left to the Harding administration, and particularly to Secretary of State Charles Evans Hughes, to reconstruct the policy of the open door and the integrity of China. For this purpose Hughes welcomed the opportunity in 1921 to assemble a nine-nation conference on Pacific questions as part of the Washington Conference on naval limitation. The Nine Power Open Door Treaty that emerged from those negotiations constituted the clearest definition and the most significant affirmation of support ever given to the principles of the open door and the integrity of China.

The Nine Power Open Door Treaty, signed on February 6, 1922, was authored primarily by Hughes and Elihu Root, both members of the American delegation to the conference. Article I of the treaty embodied the "Root formula," which the former Secretary of State introduced early in the nine-power negotiations. It was a classic statement of the American principles. The signatories pledged respect for the sovereignty, the independence, and the territorial and administrative integrity of China and engaged to maintain the principle of equal opportunity for the commerce and industry of all nations throughout China. The article also incorporated the secret protocol that had accompanied the Lansing-Ishii exchange of notes, which Hughes had revealed to Root. It pledged the powers to refrain from taking advantage of conditions in China to seek special rights or privileges that would abridge the rights of nationals of friendly states. Root balanced this restraint with the addition of a pledge to refrain from action inimical to the security of friendly states. This was undoubtedly inserted to help smooth the way to Japanese acceptance of the treaty, but it was not a novel concession. Japan had gained such an assurance from the Wilson administration in 1919 when a new four-power consortium was being organized by the United States, Britain, France, and Japan. The Japanese delegation at the Washington Conference did not regard the reaffirmation of this assurance as a significant concession or as one that could undercut the thrust and intent of the Nine Power Open Door Treaty.[28]

Other provisions of the treaty made it clear that Japan, if it observed the treaty, could no longer run roughshod over China. Article II, initially proposed by Hughes, pledged the signatories not to seek, or to support their nationals in seeking, "any arrangement which might purport to establish in favor of their interests any general superiority of rights with respect to commercial or economic development in any designated region of China." If any doubt remained about the meaning of that provision, it was resolved by Article IV, written by Root. This article committed the powers to refrain from supporting agreements by their nationals designed to create spheres of influence in China.

Considering all the setbacks that the American principles had sustained in the preceding years, the Nine Power Open Door Treaty was a remarkable achievement. It did not abolish existing spheres of influence, as China desired, but it did provide the most significant restraints against imperialist activities in China that had ever been proclaimed. By any reasonable interpretation of the treaty, the powers, including Japan, were prohibited from seeking new spheres or new rights that would enhance existing spheres. There were also other significant gains for China at the Washington Conference. Group V of the Twenty-one Demands, which in 1915 had been "postponed," were now formally withdrawn by Japan. Even more important, in Sino-Japanese negotiations conducted in Washington concurrently with the Washington Conference, Japan gave up all former German rights and interests in Shantung, retaining only a mortgage on the Tsingtao-Tsinan railway line, which was sold to China.

Why Japan was so conciliatory at the Washington Conference is still something of a mystery. Root's skillful and friendly dealing with the Japanese delegation was doubtless one reason. Also, the presence of Ambassador Shidehara Kijūrō in the Japanese delegation was an important influence for moderation. Recent scholarship also reveals that Admiral Katō Tomosaburō of the Japanese delegation strongly urged moderation on the Tokyo government.[29] A number of other things can be noted—the growing political liberalism in Japan, the disillusionment of the Japanese public and government with the Siberian intervention, Japan's pride in its new role in the League of Nations and in the international community generally. Yet these considerations do not fully explain Japan's moderate policy. The Japan of 1921–1922 still stands out in enigmatic contrast to the Japan of the Twenty-one Demands in 1915 and the Japan of the Manchurian invasion in 1931.

The victory achieved at the Washington Conference for the open door and the integrity of China unfortunately did not prove long-lived. The Washington Conference formula, by necessity, rested on a precarious balance between Japanese imperialism and Chinese nationalism, and the future character of Japanese imperialism depended in turn on the equally precarious balance of forces within Japanese politics. The work of Hughes and Root was to be shattered in the decade of the 1930s when those balances tipped. As Japan rushed headlong toward its imperial destiny in that decade, the open door and the integrity of China continued to be fundamental principles of American Far Eastern policy, but those historic principles lived on only as articles of faith, not as realistic objectives of diplomacy.

Notes

1 A. Whitney Griswold, *The Far Eastern Policy of the United States* (New York, 1938), p. 66.

2 Marilyn Blatt Young, *The Rhetoric of Empire: American China Policy, 1895–1901* (Cambridge, Mass., 1968), p. 135.

3 United States Department of State, *Papers Relating to the Foreign Relations of the United States: 1915* (Washington, D.C., 1924), pp. 114–115.

4 Hay to Roosevelt, May 1, 1902, Papers of Theodore Roosevelt, Library of Congress, Washington, D.C.

5 Raymond A. Esthus, *Theodore Roosevelt and Japan* (Seattle, Wash., 1966), pp. 25–30.

6 Durand to Lansdowne, telegram, January 23, 1905, Lansdowne Papers, F.O. 800/116, Public Record Office, London; Balfour to Lansdowne, January 24, 1905, Papers of Arthur James Balfour, British Museum, London; Lansdowne to Durand, telegram, January 25, 1905, F.O. 5/2581, Public Record Office, London; Lansdowne to Balfour, January 25, 1905, Balfour Papers.

7 Roosevelt to Cecil Spring Rice, June 13, 1904; Roosevelt to Senator Henry Cabot Lodge, June 16, 1905; Roosevelt to Kaneko, August 23, 1905; Roosevelt to Taft, December 8, 1910; Elting E. Morison, ed., *The Letters of Theodore Roosevelt*, 8 vols. (Cambridge, Mass., 1951–1954), IV, 830, 1230, 1312–1313; VII, 180–181; Takahira to Foreign Minister Komura Jutarō, September 6, 1908, Telegram Series CX, 7699–7704, Japanese Ministry of Foreign Affairs Archives, microfilm collection, Library of Congress, Washington, D.C.

8 Raymond A. Esthus, "The Changing Concept of the Open Door, 1899–1910," *Mississippi Valley Historical Review*, XLVI (1959–1960), 440–442.

9 Straight to Phillips, December 18, 1907, Willard Straight Papers, Olin Library, Cornell University, Ithaca, N.Y.

10 Memorandum by Phillips, March 6, 1908, Department of State Records, File 4002, National Archives, Washington, D.C.

11 Phillips to Rockhill, September 19, 1908, William W. Rockhill Papers, Houghton Library, Harvard University, Cambridge, Mass.

12 Esthus, *Theodore Roosevelt and Japan, op. cit.*, pp. 271–286.

13 Michael H. Hunt, *Frontier Defense and the Open Door: Manchuria in Chinese-American Relations, 1895–1911* (New Haven, Conn., 1973), pp. 202–203.

[14] Walter V. Scholes and Marie V. Scholes, *The Foreign Policies of the Taft Administration* (Columbia, Mo., 1970), pp. 166, 170–171.

[15] *Ibid.*, p. 194. Text of the secret treaty is given in Ernest B. Price, *The Russo-Japanese Treaties of 1907–1916 Concerning Manchuria and Mongolia* (Baltimore, Md., 1933), pp. 113–114.

[16] Scholes and Scholes, *op. cit.*, p. 193.

[17] Hunt, *op. cit.*, pp. 228–229.

[18] Lansing to Reinsch, November 4, 1914, United States Department of State, *Papers Relating to the Foreign Relations of the United States, 1914: Supplement* (Washington, D.C., 1928), pp. 189–190.

[19] Lansing to Bryan, March 1, 1915; Bryan to Wilson, February 22, 1915, United States Department of State, *Papers Relating to the Foreign Relations of the United States: The Lansing Papers, 1914–1920*, 2 vols. (Washington, D.C., 1939–1940), II, 405–408. Hereafter *Lansing Papers*.

[20] Bryan to the Japanese Ambassador, March 13, 1915, *Papers Relating to the Foreign Relations of the United States: 1915*, pp. 105–111.

[21] Bryan to Ambassador George W. Guthrie, telegram, March 26, 1915; Wilson to Bryan, April 14, 1915; Bryan to Reinsch, telegram, April 15, 1915; *Lansing Papers*, II, 414, 416–417; Arthur S. Link, *Wilson: The Struggle for Neutrality, 1914–1915* (Princeton, N.J., 1960), p. 289.

[22] Wilson to Bryan, May 10, 1915, *Lansing Papers*, II, 426.

[23] Bryan to Guthrie, telegram, May 11, 1915, *Papers Relating to the Foreign Relations of the United States: 1915*, p. 146.

[24] Peter Lowe, *Great Britain and Japan, 1911–1915: A Study of British Far Eastern Policy* (London, 1969), ch. 7.

[25] Reinsch to the Japanese Minister, January 3, 1917, and Lansing Memoir, January 25, 1917, United States Department of State, *Papers Relating to the Foreign Relations of the United States: 1917* (Washington, D.C., 1926), pp. 169, 117–118; Burton F. Beers, *Vain Endeavor: Robert Lansing's Attempts to End the American-Japanese Rivalry* (Durham, N.C., 1962), p. 95.

[26] Memorandum by Lansing, September 6, 1917, and Draft Note, September 26, 1917, *Lansing Papers*, II, 432–435, 440–441.

[27] Protocol to Accompany Exchange of Notes Between the Secretary of State and the Japanese Ambassador on Special Mission (Ishii), November 2, 1917, *Lansing Papers*, II, 450–451.

[28] Thomas H. Buckley, *The United States and the Washington Conference, 1921–1922* (Knoxville, Tenn., 1970), pp. 152–154.

[29] Roger Dingman, *Power in the Pacific: The Origins of Naval Arms Limitation, 1914–1922* (Chicago, 1976), pp. 211–212.

Readings and Sources

Beers, Burton F., *Vain Endeavor: Robert Lansing's Attempts to End the American-Japanese Rivalry* (Durham, N.C., 1962). This study contains the most thorough coverage of Lansing's role in the formulation of Far Eastern policy.

Buckley, Thomas H., *The United States and the Washington Conference, 1921–1922* (Knoxville, Tenn., 1970). Buckley gives the most recent and well-balanced account of the negotiation of the Nine Power Open Door Treaty.

Campbell, Charles S., Jr., *Special Business Interests and the Open Door Policy* (New Haven, Conn., 1951). This volume analyzes the influence of business interests, such as the American Asiatic Association, on the shaping of open door policy during the McKinley administration.

Curry, Roy W., *Woodrow Wilson and Far Eastern Policy, 1913–1921* (New York, 1957). This is a comprehensive and thoughtful account of Wilson's Far Eastern policy.

Dingman, Roger, *Power in the Pacific: The Origins of Naval Arms Limitation, 1914–1922* (Chicago, 1976). Dingman gives the most revealing analysis of Japanese policy decisions relating to the Washington Conference.

Esthus, Raymond A., *Theodore Roosevelt and Japan* (Seattle, Wash., 1966). This study is useful particularly for the open door policy during the Russo-Japanese War and the negotiation of the Root-Takahira exchange of notes.

Fifield, Russell H., *Woodrow Wilson and the Far East: The Diplomacy of the Shantung Question* (New York, 1952). This is the standard account of the Shantung issue.

Griswold, A. Whitney, *The Far Eastern Policy of the United States* (New York, 1938). Griswold's classic treatment has been superseded by later studies, but it is valuable for the Hippisley-Rockhill correspondence of 1899, in which the open door notes were formulated.

Hunt, Michael H., *Frontier Defense and the Open Door: Manchuria in Chinese-American Relations, 1895–1911* (New Haven, Conn., 1973). This perceptive account uses Chinese as well as Western sources.

Israel, Jerry, *Progressivism and the Open Door: America and China, 1905–1921* (Pittsburgh, Pa., 1971). This book represents a new left interpretation of the China policy of Roosevelt, Taft, and Wilson.

Langer, William L., *The Diplomacy of Imperialism, 1890–1902*, 2nd edition (New York, 1956). Langer gives the most thorough account of the acquisition of naval bases and spheres of influence in China.

Link, Arthur S., *Wilson: The Struggle for Neutrality, 1914–1915* (Princeton, N.J., 1960). This volume of Link's biographical study gives the best account available of the United States policy regarding the Twenty-one Demands.

Lowe, Peter, *Great Britain and Japan, 1911–1915: A Study of British Far Eastern Policy* (London, 1969). This excellent analysis of Britain's role in the crisis over the Twenty-one Demands supplements treatments of the American reaction.

McClellan, Robert, *Heathen Chinee: A Study of American Attitudes Toward China, 1890–1905* (Columbus, Ohio, 1970). McClellan analyzes American attitudes toward the Chinese as well as official policy.

McCormick, Thomas J., *China Market: America's Quest for Informal Empire, 1893–1901* (Chicago, 1967). This new left interpretation of open door policy emphasizes the consistency rather than the confusion in American policy.

Scholes, Walter V., and Marie V. Scholes, *The Foreign Policies of the Taft Administration* (Columbia, Mo., 1970). This book gives the most thorough account of dollar diplomacy in China.

Varg, Paul A., *The Making of a Myth: The United States and China, 1897–1912* (East Lansing, Mich., 1968). Varg examines American images of China as revealed in business, missionary, and general periodicals.

Vevier, Charles, *The United States and China, 1906–1913: A Study of Finance and Diplomacy* (New Brunswick, N.J., 1955). This study is especially useful for the role of Willard Straight.

Young, Marilyn Blatt, *The Rhetoric of Empire: American China Policy, 1895–1901* (Cambridge, Mass., 1968). This book contains the most extensive account of the background and enunciation of the open door and integrity of China policy.

Chapter Four

Sino-Japanese-American Relations During the Paris Peace Conference of 1919

BY DAVID F. TRASK

Despite the best efforts of President Woodrow Wilson to bring coherence and fixity of purpose into American policy in East Asia, that policy remained out of consonance with contemporary political realities, as the diplomacy at the Paris Peace Conference of 1919 illustrated. In Paris, American policy on the open door and the integrity of China of necessity was compromised amid the crosscurrents of politics and the maneuvers of great power diplomacy. Revolution and weakness in China, modernization and nationalism in Japan, ambition and idealism in the United States—all these came together during the World War in an imposing demonstration of the close connections between the internal dynamics of individual states, the affairs of a given geographic region, and the grand international concerns of the world powers. The United States required a policy toward China that would accord with effective policy elsewhere in Asia—notably in Japan—as well as with concerns outside the region; but Wilson's efforts never met this requirement. Circumstances forced change and compromise in his policy in East Asia, and ultimately frustrated his intentions.

When Japanese diplomats arrived at Paris in 1919 to confirm gains their country had made during the First World War (gains ostensibly at the expense of Germany but actually of

China), a notable wrangle materialized to test American policy and challenge China's sovereignty. The Chinese delegation at the peace conference relied heavily on American assistance to thwart the pretensions of Japan. During the preceding year President Woodrow Wilson had broadly advertised his support for the idea of national self-determination, an action that evidently committed him to an anti-Japanese course. On July 4, 1918, for example, he argued that the peace conference should resolve disputes "upon the basis of the free acceptance of that settlement by the people immediately concerned, and not upon the basis of the material interest or advantage of any other nation or people which may desire a different settlement for the sake of its own influence or mastery." Wilson's forthright commitment to self-determination appeared to preclude Japan's acquisition of Shantung province, a coastal portion of mainland China. Before the war Germany had developed a sphere of influence in that locale based on a leasehold around Kiaochow Bay, but Japan seized control of the region in 1914. This conquest inaugurated further Japanese initiatives, which by war's end seriously compromised the sovereignty of China.

Before examining the Shantung dispute at the Paris Peace Conference, it is useful to trace developments in East Asia during the preceding years of war. At the outset of negotiations in Paris it became apparent that Japan had emerged from the world conflict in a position to challenge America's support of China. The Shantung settlement of April 1919 came after a sharp diplomatic struggle between the United States and Japan that eventually revealed the gap between Wilsonian aspirations and mundane political conditions.

I

Shortly after the First World War erupted in August 1914, when Japan honored its obligations under the Anglo-Japanese Alliance and joined the Allied coalition against the Central

Powers, it seemed to many that Japan was more at war with China than with Germany. Japanese troops soon landed in China's Shantung province and seized the German leasehold at Kiaochow Bay, the key to a sphere of influence extending deeply into the interior and including railways and mines. Meanwhile the Japanese navy occupied Germany's insular possessions in the Pacific Ocean north of the equator—the Marshalls, Carolines, and Marianas. These unexpected accomplishments portended difficulties for the United States. Japanese retention of Shantung province would violate the territorial integrity of China. Furthermore, should Tokyo annex the mid-Pacific islands, the Japanese navy would acquire bases lying directly across America's maritime communications to the western Pacific, thus posing a strategic threat not only to the Philippines but to commercial relations with all parts of East Asia.

This disturbing trend continued when, early in 1915, Japan strengthened its grip on Shantung province and abridged Chinese sovereignty in numerous other ways. On January 18, 1915, the so-called Twenty-one Demands, which required that China acquiesce in the expansion of Japanese influence not only in Shantung province but in Mongolia, Manchuria, and central China, were presented to Peking. The Chinese government, unstable and lacking dependable allies, was hard pressed to resist these extortionate propositions. Group V of the Demands would have established a virtual protectorate over China. Yüan Shih-k'ai, President of the weak Chinese regime that had replaced the Manchu dynasty after the revolution of 1911, could do little except delay, hoping against hope that friendly powers would come to his defense.

Since all the important Western countries except the United States were deeply engaged in the European war, Yüan looked to Washington to maintain China's independence and integrity, but his hopes were disappointed. On March 13, 1915, the United States protested the Twenty-one Demands but at the same time made a damaging concession. Secretary of State William Jennings Bryan's note conceded that "territorial contiguity creates special relations between Japan and [Shantung province, southern Manchuria, and eastern Mongolia]," a view that appeared to undermine the territorial integrity of China. The American note had little effect in Tokyo; it did not mention methods of helping China if Japan refused to change its policy. Tired of Chinese foot-dragging, the Ōkuma government presented an ultimatum to China on May 7. Two days later Yüan accepted all the Japanese demands except those in Group V. On May 25 China signed a number of international engagements—two treaties and thirteen notes—that provided among other things for the return of Shantung province to China at some future date in exchange for a Japanese sphere of influence there. Although couched in language designed to soften the blow to China, these arrangements foreshadowed a truly extensive violation of the open door principles.

Seemingly forthright American pronouncements thinly disguised the fact that Washington had no intention of taking effective action to curb Tokyo. Secretary Bryan announced a doctrine of nonrecognition on May 13, 1915: The American government could not recognize a settlement "impairing the treaty rights of the United States or its citizens in China, the political or territorial integrity of the Republic of China, or the international policy commonly known as the open door policy." Unfortunately for China and for the open door policy, other international questions held higher priorities, among them an imbroglio with Mexico stemming from the revolution in that country and a dispute with the European belligerents over violations of neutral rights on the high seas. Moreover, public opinion in the United States showed no disposition to support measures more strenuous than ringing statements of principle. Perhaps the most intriguing reaction was that of Woodrow Wilson, who referred to the episode as a "whole suspicious business." Still, the President proved unwilling at this time to stand firmly against Japanese aggression in China.

Events within China also diminished the possibilities for a strong American stand for China and against Japan. Soon after these events China's politics disintegrated into civil chaos, especially after Yüan Shih-k'ai attempted to make himself emperor. Dissidents in south China based in Canton openly defied the central government at Peking, evidence that national authority had vanished. After Yüan died unexpectedly in June 1916, a successor government attempted to unite the country, but representatives of the Canton faction, reflecting the views of the anti-Japanese Kuomintang party, soon quarreled with the military leaders who controlled the northern provinces of China, and the attempt at reunification failed miserably. China then entered into "the era of warlords." For more than a decade thereafter, local military chieftains dominated the countryside; effective central government did not revive in China until the rise of Chiang Kai-shek in the late 1920s. Peking provided nominal Chinese representation at international negotiations, but the lack of firm leadership greatly facilitated the expansionist projects of Japan in East Asia, especially while the First World War absorbed the energies of the great Western powers.

The war continued to provide opportunities to Japan, and exigencies to the United States and other Western allies. Early in 1917 Japan moved efficiently to strengthen its claims to the areas it had conquered in 1914–1915. Tokyo took advantage of two dramatic events—the beginning of Russia's revolution and Germany's resumption of unrestricted submarine warfare—to extract important concessions from the European allies. The newly installed government of General Terauchi Masatake sought specific support for expansionist policies, exploiting fears in London and Paris that Japan might switch sides at a most important juncture in the world conflict. On February 16, 1917, the British government in a diplomatic note guaranteed support of Japan's claims not only to Shantung province but to the mid-Pacific islands north of the equator. Subsequently, on March 1, France pledged support of the Japanese desires in return for assistance from Tokyo in arranging China's entry into the war against the Central Powers. Japan made parallel but less formal agreements with the two other Entente powers, Italy and Russia.

By April 1917, when the United States declared war on Germany, Japan had developed formidable legal and political arguments to support claims both to a sphere of influence in Shantung province and to the Marshalls, Carolines, and Marianas, American disapproval notwithstanding. The treaties and notes of 1915 thoroughly compromised Chinese control of Shantung province, and the understandings of early 1917 committed the European Allies to back Japan's wishes at war's end. Although the United States did not concur in these arrangements, the world political situation from 1914 to 1917 definitely prejudiced prospects for an Asian settlement consistent with open door principles. Given the decline of European influence in the Far East and the debility of China, only an unprecedented manifestation of American concern and a demonstration of willingness to use force in support of diplomacy could have deterred Japanese aggression during the period 1914–1917. The United States, inattentive to affairs in Asia and preoccupied with the war in Europe, never considered any such initiatives.

Japan's expansionist policies reflected the impact of the First World War within that ambitious island nation. The conflict intensified nationalist emotions and stimulated economic growth, just as it enhanced the international prestige of the country. Gradually, the Shantung question gained notable economic and strategic importance; ultimately, it came to symbolize Japan's newfound power and position. Even after the fall of the militant Terauchi government in October 1918, imperialist and militarist elements within the oligarchic Japanese regime exercised great influence inside the supposedly moderate ministry of Hara Kei (Takashi).

Meanwhile, developments during the early months of 1917 forced China to reconsider its relation to the European war: Could not the war provide opportunities to China as to Japan? Li Yüan-hung, an interim president, favored continuance of neutrality, but the real ruler at Peking, a general named Tuan Ch'i-jui, thought differently. On March 14, 1917, he suspended diplomatic relations with Germany. The energetic American Minister, Paul S. Reinsch, strongly favored belligerency, although his unguarded anti-Japanese views received only lukewarm backing from Washington. In return for entry into the war the Peking government sought unsuccessfully to arrange the suspension of the Boxer indemnities, the increase of tariffs levied on imports into China, and the elimination of legation guards. All these concerns were legacies of Western inroads into China. Failure to win these concessions led the Canton dissidents, advocates of democratic parliamentarianism and opponents of Japanese expansion, to oppose war. Eventually General Tuan aligned himself against the Kuomintang, but President Li supported it. After a confusing series of events, including a bizarre but abortive restoration of the Manchu dynasty, Tuan regained control in Peking. The Kuomintang delegates in the central government withdrew to Canton and openly defied Tuan. In response to this development Tuan sought arms from Japan; he needed them to establish his authority in the south by force. This policy gave Japan further opportunities to impair Chinese sovereignty.

On August 14, 1917, Tuan's Peking government finally declared war on Germany, but China gained only one significant advantage from this step. The treaty rights of Germany and Austria-Hungary were abolished, the first successful assault on foreign privileges. Although China dispatched about 175,000 laborers to Europe and the Middle East to support the Allied and Associated powers, it sent no combat troops. Tuan used his army against the southern dissidents and Tokyo proved helpful in this regard. A special representative of General Terauchi, an agent named Nishihara, advanced numerous unsecured loans to China through the Minister of Communications, Ts'ao Ju-lin. In return Tuan signed three secret agreements on September 24, 1918, which further clouded China's title to the leasehold at Kiaochow Bay and prejudiced its chances of regaining railway and mining concessions in the interior.

As the prospects for Chinese sovereignty and democracy declined during 1917–1918, the United States failed to take an effective position against Japanese expansion because of its deep involvement in the European struggle. After America entered the World War in April 1917, Tokyo sent a diplomatic mission to Washington. At its head was the new ambassador, Count Ishii Kikujiro, eager to derive advantage from America's involvement in the global conflict. Ishii hoped to exploit the American notion advanced in 1915 that territorial contiguity between China and Japan implied special relations between those two countries. Neither President Wilson nor his Secretary of State, Robert Lansing, wished to pursue this point, but in their dealings with Ishii they found themselves without much ground for maneuver.

Both Wilson and Lansing were sincere friends of China, but they realized that serious complications might develop if the United States failed to retain the friendship of Japan during the wartime emergency. These considerations greatly influenced the Lansing-Ishii Agreement of November 2, 1917. In it the United States and Japan reaffirmed the open door principles but agreed that "Territorial propinquity creates special relations between countries. . . . Japan has special interests in China, particularly in the part to which her possessions are contiguous." Although this statement seemed merely to reiterate the concessions of May 1915, its timing implied a certain weakening of American support for China's territorial integrity. This interpretation gained spurious currency when the Japanese attempted to translate "special interests in China" as "paramount interests in China."

Lacking real negotiating strength, Lansing temporized in the hope that the American bargaining position would improve later on. To insure that Japan did not take immediate advantage of the situation, the Secretary of State negotiated a secret protocol providing that Tokyo would not exploit "present conditions to seek special rights and privileges in China which would abridge the rights of citizens or subjects of other friendly states." Nevertheless, because the protocol was not made public at the time, the negotiations of 1917 appeared to onlookers as a real American retreat. The outcome pleased Tokyo; it encouraged the thought that the United States might eventually relax its opposition to Japanese initiatives in China.

Despite preoccupation with the war in Europe, the United

States made some attempts during 1917–1918 to strengthen China's position *vis-à-vis* Japan. Although Washington encouraged China to declare war on the Central Powers, it urged the government in Peking to concentrate primarily on internal reform rather than foreign adventures. On June 4, 1917, for example, a diplomatic note placed national regeneration ahead of the war effort: "The principal necessity for China is to resume and continue her political entity and to proceed along the road of national development on which she has made such marked progress." This course required financial support of China. Accordingly, Wilson reversed his long-standing opposition to an international consortium of bankers set up to finance Chinese development. In 1913 the President had abandoned such an arrangement because it seemed to threaten Chinese sovereignty. By 1918 he realized that dependence on Japanese loans would threaten China. Therefore, on June 2, 1918, Wilson authorized Lansing to facilitate entrance of American bankers into the international consortium, at the same time insisting that the step was consistent with the open door principles. Here is a striking example of the unexpected outcomes of war; it is difficult to imagine other circumstances that could have forced the proud American President to such an about-face.

After the Bolshevik revolution took place in Russia, controversies resulting from various proposals to launch an inter-Allied intervention during 1918 reinforced the anti-Japanese tendency of American policy. The President stubbornly opposed British, French, and Japanese efforts to reconstitute the Eastern Front in Russia as a means of preventing Germany from shifting forces westward for the vital campaign in France during 1918. He had a number of reasons for his intransigence on this question, among them fear that a Japanese incursion into eastern Eurasia would compromise the future of China. By July, however, inter-Allied pressure forced the President to condone small incursions in north Russia and eastern Siberia to accomplish strictly limited purposes. Discussions with the Japanese government about landings at Vladivostok produced what Wilson construed as an understanding to send in a small number of troops to conduct carefully circumscribed operations. When the Japanese army failed to observe this arrangement, Wilson reacted bitterly, telling an adviser early in 1919 that "he did not in fact trust the Japanese, . . . he had trusted them before—in fact they had broken their agreement about Siberia. We had sent 7,000 troops to Siberia and they promised to send about the same number but had sent 70,000 and had occupied all the strategic points as far as Irkutsk, and . . . he would not trust them again." His Asian policies during the Paris Peace Conference reflected this abiding lack of trust.

In January 1918, and thereafter, President Wilson made public his war aims and peace plans in the form of the Fourteen Points and various associated principles, an initiative that appeared likely to benefit China because it rested firmly on the concept of self-determination, but prior developments had compromised the Chinese future. Japanese negotiations during 1917–1918 with China, the Entente powers, and even the United States established an imposing legal claim on Germany's sphere of influence in Shantung province and to the mid-Pacific islands occupied in 1914. Striking shifts in the East Asian balance of power resulting from events of the great war—changes quite favorable to Japan—further strengthened the bargaining power of Japanese diplomats designated to attend the Paris Peace Conference of 1919. Although anti-Japanese sentiment had flowered within the Wilson administration, the United States had not imposed really effective constraints on Tokyo's freedom of action.

During the peace negotiations at Paris a contest over control of Shantung province exposed the gap between Wilson's peace plans and the mundane political realities of East Asia. During 1919 as in 1914 the President stood firmly opposed to impairment of Chinese sovereignty and strongly in favor of democracy for both China and Japan. But if his overall objectives remained unchanged during the war, his means of achieving them altered greatly. American plans for a new world order envisioned a collective-security system rather than an old-fashioned balance of power to guarantee the sovereignty of beleaguered China and to foster democracy there. It remained to be seen whether Wilsonian hope could be translated into East Asian practice.

II

At two distinct points the conflicting claims of the Chinese and Japanese delegations to Shantung province came before the Paris Peace Conference. Late in January 1919, representatives of both nations stated their positions before the Council of Ten —a group including the heads of government and the foreign ministers from the five great powers (Britain, France, Italy, Japan, and the United States). Almost three months later, during the last two weeks of April, the Council of Four—composed of Prime Minister David Lloyd George of Great Britain, Premier Georges Clemenceau of France, Premier Vittorio Orlando of Italy, and President Wilson of the United States—finally reached a decision.

Japan sent competent diplomats to Paris. Prince Saionji Kimmochi, one of the elder statesmen of Japan, headed his country's delegation, but most of the labor in Paris fell to Count Makino Nobuaki, former Minister of Foreign Affairs, and Viscount Chinda Sutemi, Ambassador to Great Britain. Two other members, the Japanese Ambassadors to France and Italy, played subordinate roles. The negotiations constituted an important turning point in Japan's history; for the first time its spokesmen received the special treatment extended to great powers at an international conference. Nevertheless, the delegation lived in fear that diplomacy at Paris might lead to humiliations like those of 1895 and 1905. After both the Sino-Japanese War and the Russo-Japanese War, Western pressure had forced Japan to recede from advanced demands. As it turned out, Tokyo closely supervised Saionji and his colleagues, and, consequently, they did not have to take responsibility for agonizing decisions.

The situation was quite different within the talented Chinese delegation, which had considerable discretion because of weakness in Peking. Titular leadership fell to Lu Tseng-tsiang, the Foreign Minister of China, but two men who had been educated in the United States—V. K. Wellington Koo, and C. T. Wang, a representative of the provisional government at Canton—completed the delegation. During the later stages of the conference, another spokesman for southern interests, C. C. Wu, joined the group. Wang and Wu were allowed to participate because of a concurrent attempt in China to heal the split between Peking and Canton. Hsü Shih-ch'ang, who came to power in the north during September 1918, followed a policy of national reconciliation. Representatives of contending factions gathered at Shanghai during February 1919 for discussions intended to foster internal stability, a circumstance that somewhat bolstered the Chinese delegation, although it by no means disguised the homeland's disunity and weakness.

Japan entered negotiations at Paris with clear objectives and a strong bargaining position. Its delegates had instructions to take over the rights of Germany in Shantung province, to annex the Marshalls, Carolines, and Marianas, and to insert a clause in the treaty endorsing the principle of racial equality. The territorial objectives were well supported, given developments between 1914 and 1918. Diplomatic settlements with China in 1915 and 1918 and with the Entente powers and the United States in 1917 provided solid legal justification. Equally important, Tokyo exercised military control of the islands and of Shantung province.

Despite its interest in territorial demands, the Japanese delegation gave considerable attention to the issue of racial equality. This moral question generated significant political appeal because of its consistency with Wilsonian premises. Japan's drive for a ringing pronouncement of racial equality was no mere "bargaining chip" to be relinquished for some territorial concession; it reflected truly important concerns of the Japanese people and their proud leaders.

The Chinese delegation also urged specific objectives on the conference, but from the outset its position lacked solidity. China sought to recover sovereignty in Shantung province; to abrogate all treaties and agreements stemming from the Twenty-one Demands; to liquidate German and Austrian treaty rights; and to eliminate special treaty rights and privileges conceded to all other foreigners. To undermine the strong legal case of Japan, Wellington Koo argued that the Sino-Japanese agreements lacked legitimacy because they were negotiated under duress. On occasion he also cited a legal formula holding that changed circumstances can invalidate earlier agreements (*rebus sic stantibus*). These arguments allowed China to invoke Wilsonian principles, particularly self-determination, in behalf of its claims. To compensate for China's weakness at the bargaining table, Koo and Wang relied heavily upon the United States, establishing close working relations with certain advisers to the American delegation, notably Stanley K. Hornbeck and E. T. Williams, and building almost universal support among other Americans in Paris.

The peace conference first considered the conflicting desires of China and Japan during deliberations of the Council of Ten on January 27–28, 1919. On the first day Count Makino put forward Japan's claim to Germany's leased territory around Kiaochow Bay along with rail and mining concessions in Shantung. He also demanded title to the German islands in the mid-Pacific Ocean north of the equator. Wellington Koo spoke the next day, calling upon the Council to restore Germany's rights in Shantung directly to China. (Earlier Japan had promised to restore Chinese sovereignty after *first* acquiring Germany's rights.) He advanced two arguments: China's entry into the war had canceled all previous agreements with Germany; direct restitution of Shantung accorded with President Wilson's points. To these remarks Makino replied simply that Japan held the disputed territory and possessed the right to settle the future of Shantung province as it wished, presumably by direct negotiations with China after the peace treaty formally transferred Germany's rights to the Japanese government. His remarks clearly implied Japan's intention to stand firmly on the diplomatic commitments of 1915, 1917, and 1918. Koo could only restate his argument that China's declaration of war had abrogated the Sino-Japanese agreements.

After this initial debate the Shantung issue did not surface again in the Council of Ten, or in its successor, the Council of Four, until April 1919, but during the interim both China and Japan pressed their views on other matters. Tokyo's efforts to obtain a legally binding statement of racial equality ultimately came to nothing. This campaign encountered vociferous objections from Prime Minister E. M. Hughes of Australia. Acting for those who opposed the racial equality clause, he fought the measure in various forums. In this single instance Wilson supported Japan, but to facilitate agreement he eventually opted for compromise, namely a pronouncement of principle that would not be legally binding. Eventually the conference refused to accept even this arrangement. On April 11, during a session of the League of Nations Commission, eleven of seventeen member nations voted in favor of the racial equality clause, but the presiding officer, Wilson, ruled that the measure had failed because unanimity was required to permit inclusion of any article in the covenant. Japan now had to prepare its actions when the covenant minus the racial equality clause came before a plenary session of the peace conference. Would Makino and Chinda spurn membership in the League of Nations because the peace conference had failed to endorse racial equality?

While the Japanese delegation fought doggedly for racial equality, it also pressed a claim to the Marshalls, Carolines, and Marianas. Although Japan was forced to accept the mandate principle, which obligated colonial powers to prepare dependencies for eventual self-government and to refrain from fortifying them, no effective opposition materialized to block the desired annexation. President Wilson could not successfully deny Japanese aspirations to the mid-Pacific islands, but he recognized the adverse strategic import of the outcome, telling one adviser as early as January 1919: "These islands lie athwart the path from Hawaii to the Philippines, . . . They were nearer Hawaii than the Pacific coast . . . they could be fortified and made naval bases by Japan; . . . indeed they were of little use for anything else and . . . we have no naval base except Guam [in that zone.]"

The Chinese delegation maintained active propaganda in behalf of its desires. Koo and his colleagues produced reams of documents dealing with Shantung province, the rights of the Central Powers in China, and the unequal treaty provisions—especially extraterritoriality, tariff regulation, location of foreign troops on Chinese territory, and foreign control of communications. This activity conveyed the impression that China enjoyed a strong bargaining position, but the real situation became apparent when a showdown took place in April.

Wilson's pro-Chinese orientation in Paris revealed itself at every stage in the negotiations. A. Whitney Griswold aptly summarized America's Asian policy during the peace conference. The United States intended to prevent Japanese domination of the Chinese economy by participating in an international consortium set up to finance various development projects. Meanwhile, the presence of American troops in Siberia would preclude Japanese expansion in that unsettled region. To further justice and curb Japan, Shantung province was to be returned directly to China. International endorsement of collective security and nonaggression in the League covenant would protect China and deter Japan indefinitely. Public opinion in the United States, insofar as it had formed, definitely approved of anti-Japanese actions. Among the American peace commissioners in Paris only the supple Edward M. House—better known as Colonel House—appeared willing to compromise support of China.

As late as April 15 President Wilson expressed strong approbation of the Chinese claims. Once again he voiced suspicion that Asian rather than European problems might soon constitute the most imposing threats to peace. "My sympathies are on the side of China," he said, "and we must not forget that the greatest future dangers for the world may present themselves in the Pacific." What exactly did the President have in mind? Surely he had reference to the possibility, alluded to earlier in this essay, that Japan and Russia might attempt to expand at the expense of China and thus mount a most serious threat to peace and progress throughout East Asia.

From late January to mid-April 1919, several initiatives contrary to Japan's plans for Shantung province were broached in Paris, and one of them received some attention from the Council of Ten. On April 15, 1919, Secretary of State Robert Lansing proposed that the five great powers become trustees for Shantung. Presumably the trustees would receive and dispose of Germany's rights rather than either China or Japan doing so alone. President Wilson seized upon this idea, developing it in the Council of Four on April 18. "We should advise the Japanese to be generous toward China," he argued, "and [we] should promise them, if they follow our advice, that we will facilitate their peaceful relations with the Chinese Republic." He wanted to go further. "What would enable us to speak with authority would be an announcement that we ourselves are renouncing our zones of influence in China." In this respect the President asked the French and British to make material sacrifices. The United States would relinquish nothing since it possessed no sphere of influence in China.

What lay behind the President's search for a diplomatic settlement favorable to China but acceptable to Japan? Once more he expatiated on his suspicion that future threats to peace would most likely rise in the Far East. "I fear, from this direction, great dangers for the world if we are not very careful." He felt that, when "Bolshevik fever" had been cured in Europe, war would not visit that continent for a long time to come, but the situation in Asia struck him differently. "I would compare the hidden seeds of conflict which are developing here to those sparks, concealed beneath a thick bed of leaves, which creep along for months and spread little by little, invisible, until the moment when, suddenly, there bursts out one of these great forest fires that we sometimes see in America." This conflagration had to be avoided; otherwise the future would shape itself along lines very different from the Wilsonian scenario.

Here, then, was further explanation of what lay behind Wilson's earlier concern about the Far East. He feared that Japanese and Russian efforts to expand at the expense of China would unsettle not only East Asia but the entire world. This central theme—worry about imperialistic enterprises not only violating the open door principles but subverting the broader ideals imbedded in the covenant of the League—certainly dwarfed other considerations. Wilson was firmly convinced that the world could avoid future warfare only if the nations abided by his prescriptions for a progressive but stable world order, none of which seemed more important than those designed to eliminate imperialism and militarism.

By April 1919, disputation among the contending delegations over many questions besides Shantung province—among them proposed amendments to the covenant of the League, Italian territorial claims, and military terms to be imposed on the defeated powers—had engendered an atmosphere of crisis in Paris. Some observers predicted that the conference would break up without reaching agreement. The moment was excruciating for President Wilson. He believed firmly that his plans for a new world order depended upon universal membership in the League of Nations. Would important countries such as Japan and Italy refuse to join the organization if the Treaty of Versailles did not recognize their national claims?

This consideration made Wilson vulnerable in certain bargaining situations because some countries sensed an opportunity to barter their membership in the League for American concessions that violated the Fourteen Points and associated pronouncements. In some situations Wilson accepted the adverse consequences of insisting on his own views. For example, he remained intransigent in rejecting Italy's overblown demands, even after Premier Orlando bolted the conference in protest. The Japanese claims posed for Wilson a situation roughly analogous to the Italian imbroglio. If Japan forced him to choose between anti-imperialism and universal participation in the League, how would he react? The answer came after intensive discussions in the Council of Four.

III

The climactic negotiation of the Shantung question began on April 21, 1919, when Wilson reported to his colleagues an interesting conversation with Makino and Chinda concerning the Japanese claims. He had proposed a five-power trusteeship for Shantung province, but the Japanese delegates continued to insist on direct cession of Germany's rights. He was told in no uncertain terms that "the powers should trust Japan to carry out her bargain with China." Despite this statement the President was encouraged because the Japanese appeared willing to consider general abandonment of all special foreign rights in China, particularly those that buttressed spheres of influence—the right of extraterritoriality and the right to station troops. Looking at the bright side, Wilson opined: "It would be a great thing if we could get rid of the right of Japan to maintain troops in Kiau-chau."

At this point the Japanese home government took a most important action, sending a blunt telegraphic instruction to the delegation in Paris designed to govern all of its later negotiations. Germany must cede all its rights in Shantung province directly to Japan; the leasehold at Kiaochow Bay would be returned to China later. The foreign office stated that this decision was final; it would consider no change. A chilling directive concluded the communication: "In case our proposal is not approved . . . do not sign the Covenant of the League of Nations and advise us to that effect." This hard line reflected confidence that Tokyo possessed considerable leverage in Paris. On the same day Makino restated the Japanese position in the Council of Four, methodically refuting all the Chinese arguments in behalf of direct restitution. He had no thought of varying from the home government's desires.

What of the arrangements Japan had made with the Entente powers early in 1917? When Lloyd George reviewed these agree-

ments, he attributed them to the need at a critical moment during the war to obtain naval assistance from Japan. He did not
mention the Western fear at the time that Japan might have
been contemplating a reversal of alliances. Lloyd George and
Clemenceau showed no inclination to repudiate their wartime
commitments despite evidence that both leaders disliked Japan's
enterprises in China. This attitude naturally pleased nations such
as Australia and New Zealand, which sought other pieces of
German territory. Wilson was disadvantaged in dealing with
the understandings of 1917 because one of the war aims of the
Allies had been to uphold the sanctity of treaties, a principle
that Germany had violated when it invaded Belgium in 1914.
This consideration lent additional strength to the Japanese
bargaining position. The delegation at Paris accurately appraised
the Entente powers in a message sent at this time to Tokyo:
"There is no doubt that both England and France are taking the
attitude of honestly carrying out their official promises to us
and that the only question that remains is how strongly they will
maintain this attitude against the opposition of America." Here,
concluded the message, lay "the key point of the matter."

On April 22, 1919, President Wilson summarized his view
of East Asian relations. He feared that Japan was giving more
thought to its rights than to its duties. "The central idea of the
League of Nations," he continued, "was that states must support
each other even when their interests were not involved." He
hoped that Japan would become the expositor of the new
world order in the Far East. Once again Wilson expressed his
desire that the great powers liquidate their special treaty rights
in China; otherwise the Far East might enter an era of dangerous
instability. "There was a lot of combustible material in China
and if flames were put to it the fire could not be quenched for
China had a population of four hundred million people. It was
symptoms of that," he concluded, "which filled him with anxiety." Nevertheless, Wilson had to acknowledge the force of
European arguments concerning the sanctity of treaties, even if
he knew of cases "where treaties ought not to have been en-

tered into." Presumably he referred not only to the agreements between China and Japan but to those between the Entente powers and Japan.

For its part the Chinese delegation recounted familiar arguments in a message of April 23, 1919, while the Council of Four prepared to make its decision. This document, a transparent effort to rekindle American support, dwelt particularly on the conflict between the compromising treaties and the Fourteen Points. Fair treatment of China would insure peace in Asia for a half century, but if the conference endorsed the illegitimate Sino-Japanese treaties of 1915 and 1918, "it may be sowing seeds of a grave discord in the years soon to come." The Chinese people might "attribute the failure not so much to Japan's insistence on her own claims as to the attitude of the West, which declined to lend a helping hand to China merely because some of its leading Powers had privately pledged to help Japan." Here was an obvious appeal to President Wilson, one that emphasized views the American himself had expressed during the controversy over the Asian settlement. Unfortunately for China this strategy did not carry the day.

At length Lloyd George, Clemenceau, and Wilson developed a scheme to have Arthur Balfour, the British Foreign Minister, make an arrangement that would satisfy Japan but bear as lightly as possible on China. The British wanted to recognize the exalted position of Japan in the Far East but at the same time to insure that China eventually would regain nominal sovereignty in Shantung province. This formula scarcely disguised surrender to Japan, but Wilson made no objection.

Wilson had come to the end of his rope; surely, as his press adviser, Ray Stannard Baker, expressed it, he had reached his Gethsemane. If the President persisted in his pro-Chinese policy, would Japan join Italy in a boycott of the proposed League? Seeking some way out of a truly agonizing situation, Wilson took the unusual step of consulting his fellow plenipotentiaries in Paris. Three of the four other peace commissioners—Lansing, Henry White, and General Tasker H. Bliss—opposed concessions to Japan. Only Colonel House countenanced a retreat.

After Balfour consulted the Japanese delegation, he reported the outcome. If Japan received the rights of Germany in Shantung province, it would later restore Chinese sovereignty and retain only the economic rights Germany had possessed—a concession in the port city of Tsingtao, railway rights, and mining privileges. If the Council acceded to Japan's desires, Makino and Chinda intimated that they would drop their demands that the conference insert in the Covenant of the League a legally binding commitment to racial equality.

President Wilson finally made his decision; he accepted the Balfour formula with the proviso that Japan confine its permanent demands to economic matters. He came to believe that the Japanese delegation would indeed reject a treaty that omitted a Shantung settlement acceptable to Tokyo. To ease the disappointment of China, he gave notice that, when the League began operations, he would seek an end to the right of extraterritoriality in China.

After Wilson's change of front Balfour insisted that "the main doubts and difficulties" had been disposed of, hoping to insure that during a plenary meeting of the peace conference scheduled for that very day, April 28, 1919, the Japanese delegation would recede from its advanced position on racial equality. When Makino addressed the full conference, he reviewed Japan's efforts in behalf of racial equality and indicated his intention not to press the matter further. Despite "poignant regret" at the outcome of the debate over racial equality, Japan had finally traded off the principle to obtain a favorable Shantung settlement.

On April 29, 1919, General Bliss, acting for White and Lansing as well, sent a powerful protest to Wilson critical of the Shantung settlement, one that relied on familiar moral arguments. "If it be right for a policeman, who recovers your purse, to keep the contents and claim that he had fulfilled his duty on returning the empty purse, then Japan's conduct may be tolerated." This comment pointed up the emptiness of Japan's agreement to restore sovereignty over Shantung province to China. Real power would flow from the arrangements permitting

Japan to develop a sphere of influence. "If it be right for Japan to annex the territory of an Ally, then it cannot be wrong for Italy to retain Fiume taken from the enemy." In these words Bliss noted evident inconsistency in the President's actions at Paris. "If we support Japan's claim, we abandon the democracy of China to the domination of the Prussianized militarism of Japan." Bliss implied that Wilson had failed to honor his own anti-militarism. The letter concluded dramatically: "It can't be right to do wrong even to make peace. Peace is desirable, but there are things dearer than peace, justice and freedom." It is difficult to identify a more powerful dissent from a presidential decision during the Wilson administration, an indication of the intense feelings surrounding the American retreat.

Colonel House, predictably, reacted quite differently; his soothing letter to the President helped assuage the pain of General Bliss's tongue-lashing. Although he agreed that the outcome was "all bad," he thought it no more compromising than many other settlements, and it might prepare the way for justice later on. He wanted to move beyond the petty disputes of the moment: "I feel . . . that we had best clean up a lot of old rubbish with the least friction, and let the League of Nations and the new era do the rest." House held out the prospect that temporary wrong could be redressed in the future: "England, France, and Japan ought to get out of China, and perhaps they will [leave] later if enough pressure is brought through public opinion as expressed in the League of Nations." And so the matter rested.

Despite yeoman efforts by the Chinese delegation the Balfour arrangement entered into the Treaty of Versailles. Although its provisions reflected Wilson's efforts to sugarcoat the outcome by limiting Japan to economic concessions, it was impossible to conceal the patent reality that Japan had gained a signal diplomatic victory. Articles 156 and 157 provided for the return of Shantung province to China after Japan received Germany's rights there. Japan would retain only those rights of Germany that concerned railways, mining, and the settlement in the city of Tsingtao. Restrictions were placed on Japan's use of police in Shantung province, a face-saving arrangement intended to underline opposition to a Japanese military presence. On June 28, 1919, when the peace conference convened to sign the Versailles Treaty, the Chinese delegation remained aloof. Fortunately this act did not keep China out of the League, because its representatives later approved treaties for the other Central Powers (except Turkey), which included the Covenant of the League and abrogated German and Austrian rights in China.

The outcome in Paris did not pass unremarked in China. On May 4, 1919, just a few days after the decision in the Council of Four, some three thousand angry students gathered in Peking at the Gate of Heavenly Peace. Their wrath soon turned against the Minister of Communications, Ts'ao Ju-lin, who with the head of the Currency Bureau, Lu Tsang-yu, and the Minister to Japan, Chang Tsung-hsiang, formed a pro-Japanese cabal inside the shaky Chinese government. When rioters discovered Chang hiding in Ts'ao's home, they beat him so badly that he required hospitalization. Student demonstrations soon materialized elsewhere, notably in urban centers such as Shanghai, Nanking, and Canton. On May 15, 1919, an "Internal Peace Conference" met at Shanghai—called to halt a virtual civil war between the central government and the separatist movement in southern China—but it broke up in confusion after the dissidents demanded that the Peking regime abrogate certain secret treaties with Japan and repudiate the Treaty of Versailles. At the same time a boycott of foreign products began at Shanghai. Like the student protests, this manifestation spread quickly. By June 10 the agitators had accomplished two important goals: Ts'ao and his henchmen had been forced from power, and the Chinese delegation at the Paris Peace Conference had received instructions to repudiate the offending treaty.

The "May Fourth Movement" in China, an intellectual and political upheaval stressing modernization, national regeneration, and hatred of Westerners, flowed from these events and vastly influenced the course of Chinese affairs during the succeeding decade. The ferment of the day stimulated not only the Nationalist party of Chiang Kai-shek but also an internal Communist movement. For the moment these natural rivals could unite against foreign incursions. Their contest for power would culminate only when, once again, Western influence in East Asia declined because of another massive world conflict.

Why did Wilson suddenly reverse his China policy in April 1919 after stoutly resisting the pretensions of Japan for several months? Surely he did so because he became convinced that Japan would make good its threat to boycott the League of Nations unless its desires concerning Shantung province were included in the Treaty of Versailles. Wilson also bowed to Japan's demands for a mandate over the Marshalls, Carolines, and Marianas, an undesirable concession somewhat mitigated by constraints imposed on the mandatory powers. Japan and America agreed on one important issue raised at Paris—both supported racial equality—but Australia and other countries managed to block its endorsement. Russell Fifield, the leading authority, has aptly confirmed the accuracy of Wilson's assumption that Japan would remain outside the League unless the peace conference accepted its demands on China, but he has also showed that the President erred in his belief that China would eventually receive justice at the hands of the League.

Wilson acted against his strong pro-Chinese inclination because Japan possessed a strong bargaining position at Paris. The Middle Kingdom was weak, whereas the Land of the Rising Sun successfully rode the wave of modernization. Wilson had to consider the consequences, should he support China to the bitter end, not only for the League of Nations but for America's security in the Pacific Ocean. He certainly aspired to act not only in accord with the open door principles but with his own blueprint for a new order of world politics. When he came to the moment of decision between Japan and China in 1919, he countenanced short-run injustice in the name of what he hoped would be long-term equity. In this instance as in others the President looked ahead to the healing functions of the League as a means of insuring a just and lasting peace. Only for such a great end would Woodrow Wilson even momentarily compromise the principles for which he contended so strenuously.

Some recent investigators suggest that racism dictated Wilson's decision at Paris, but available evidence does not substantiate this view. It is true that in February 1917 the Secretary of Agriculture, David F. Houston, recorded in his diary a presidential comment to the Cabinet that the United States might have to remain outside of the European conflict to insure against future dangers in Asia. Neutrality might be called for "to keep the white race or part of it strong enough to meet the yellow race—Japan, for instance, in alliance with Russia, dominating China." Although this speculation of Wilson may have reflected underlying racist sentiment, he embraced the principle of racial equality at Paris and constantly voiced support of China's aspirations. No one has been able to show that he was insincere in these actions. The President undoubtedly entertained conceptions of Caucasian superiority, and certainly he worried about dangers to "white" civilization that might emanate from the East. Wilson and many of his contemporaries accepted the prevailing Social Darwinism of the day, which assigned Orientals an inferior place in a spurious hierarchy of racial competence, but this sad misconception did not prevent him and practically all other Americans from expressing continual and sincere sympathy for China, a proclivity consistent with an abstract principle (self-determination) and a concrete self-interest (security in the Pacific). Those who insist that racial prejudice determined the President's behavior ignore the patent fact that in choosing between the Japanese and Chinese claims at Paris he was deciding between two Oriental cultures. Had Wilson resisted the Japanese claims, would later critics accuse him of racial prejudice because he acted against the desires of a "yellow" country—Japan? It seems unlikely. If abstract philosophic assumptions influenced Wilson's behavior at Paris or that of other members of the American Commission to Negotiate Peace, they tended to reinforce sympathy for one "yellow" nation, China, and antipathy toward another.

Wilson's goals in East Asia remained constant during the period 1914–1919. He favored Chinese independence and the growth of democracy throughout the region; he became more and more committed to these ends as the First World War ran its course.

But circumstances—the realities of internal Chinese and Japanese affairs, regional opportunities open to Japan during the European war, and the tightening relationship between East Asian stability and world order—changed Wilson's conception of how to accomplish his purposes. By 1919 he had become an advocate of collective security, and he based the League of Nations Covenant on this technique. Wilson underestimated the imperialist tendencies of Japan and overestimated the potential for democracy in China. To his credit, he foresaw the possibility of truly destabilizing developments in East Asia if the negotiations of 1919 did not accomplish their purpose. Perhaps his greatest error was to assume that his countrymen shared his views. When the Senate failed to accept the Treaty of Versailles, it dealt a crippling blow to Wilson's plans for a new world order. Thereafter the United States was precluded from cooperating with friendly powers to make good the promises to China in the Treaty of Versailles.

And so Woodrow Wilson and his associates at Paris failed to forestall the growth of serious Asian threats to world order and progress. China's anti-foreignism, instability, and revolution; Japan's pan-Asianism, militarism, and autocracy: These would endure and ultimately would threaten American security and world peace.

Readings and Sources

Beers, Burton F., *Vain Endeavor: Robert Lansing's Attempts to End the American-Japanese Rivalry* (Durham, N.C., 1962). This model monograph delineates the role of the Secretary of State.

Duus, Peter, *Party Rivalry and Political Change in Taisho, Japan.* (Cambridge, Mass., 1938). This study is one of the most useful general works treating the influence of Japanese domestic politics in foreign affairs.

Fifield, Russell, *Woodrow Wilson and the Far East: The Diplomacy of the Shantung Question* (Hamden, Conn., 1965; originally published 1952). The present essay largely accepts the scholarship in this book, which is by far the most important work on the American role.

Foreign Relations of the United States (Washington, D.C., various). These documentary collections published by the Department of State provide the principal published source for materials on Sino-American relations during the First World War. The series includes, besides the annual publications for 1914 through 1919, special supplements on the war for 1917 and 1918 and a further, thirteen-volume set covering the Paris Peace Conference. Here can be found the minutes of the Council of Four, the Council of Ten, and the League of Nations Commission.

Israel, Jerry, *Progressivism and the Open Door: America and China, 1905–1921* (Pittsburgh, Pa., 1971). This volume reflects recent interpretation by younger scholars.

La Fargue, Thomas Edward, *China and the World War* (New York, 1973; originally published 1937). Like many other volumes written in the 1930s about China, this one remains useful.

Mantoux, Paul, *Paris Peace Conference 1919: Proceedings of the Council of Four (March 24–April 28)* (Geneva, Switzerland, 1964). The notes of the French interpreter for the Council contain an alternate published record of its proceedings.

Pollard, Robert T., *China's Foreign Relations, 1917–1931* (New York, 1933). This book provides a useful overview within which to pursue special topics.

Reinsch, Paul S., *An American Diplomat in China* (Taipei, Taiwan, 1967; originally published 1922). This careful memoir remains highly informative.

T'ang Leang-Li, *The Inner History of the Chinese Revolution* (London, 1930). Although dated, this study is not without usefulness and should not be overlooked.

Tatsuji Takeuchi, *War and Diplomacy in the Japanese Empire* (Garden City, N.Y., 1935). It is interesting to note that some of the first books on topics germane to the present essay were essentially sound and, like this one, remain useful.

Chapter Five

The Far East in American Strategy, 1948-1951

BY THOMAS H. ETZOLD

I

The long-standing ambiguity of American security concerns in the Far East deserves attention in the 1970s because of the high importance of those concerns in Asian international affairs in the last three decades. The facts of American military presence and commitment in Korea, Taiwan, and Japan, the uncertainty attaching to American interests and intentions, the apparently pointless intervention in Vietnam: these have filled China's leaders with apprehension and the American public with dismay. In turn, such emotions have stimulated antagonism in the relations of China with the United States. Within the United States, these same emotions have led to contradiction: resurgent isolationism, a legacy of the Vietnam experience; and, concurrently, naïve hope for a greatly improved and expanded relationship with the People's Republic of China.

The foundation of both the facts and the uncertainties of American security concerns in Asia since World War II was established in the evolution of an American strategic concept for Asia in the years 1948 to 1951. Explanation of the ambiguity of American intentions and of the paradox of American posture in the Far East in regard to security concerns depends on assessment of the interaction of three factors: (1) postwar American attempts to organize disparate global interests into a coherent scheme of policy and strategy; (2) the effects of the civil war in China on the evolving scheme; and (3) the influence, both regional and extraregional, of the outbreak of conflict in Korea on the new strategic concepts of American military and political leaders.

Because it is no accident that an era of improvement in Sino-American relations has coincided with a time of devolution in American military presence in Asia, it is all the more paradoxical that American military posture in the Far East, as developed from 1948 through the summer of 1951, *was* accidental. That posture was far more the result of time and circumstance than a manifestation of evolving American conceptions about the significance and role of the Far East in American security. In 1947 and 1948 military and political leaders joined in pronouncing Korea indefensible and in planning for withdrawal of American troops. From 1948 onward, American policymakers at the highest levels came to believe that Communism in China was an annoyance, but not a threat, to the United States. They even anticipated with calm, though not happiness, a Chinese Communist seizure of Taiwan. With deliberation, these same officials declared it unnecessary to retain American military bases in Taiwan or Japan. By January of 1950, with American troops out of Korea, the Secretary of State, Dean G. Acheson, in a speech to the National Press Club could omit Korea from the "defensive perimeter" of the United States. As has become only too evident over succeeding decades, conflict in Korea led to an American military stance in Asia that was at once unexpected, unintended, and unwanted.

II

In contrast to the years before the Second World War, after 1945 America's political and military concerns related systematically and sometimes closely to interests elsewhere. Before that war the United States had at will or whim enjoyed the luxury of associating or dissociating policies in distant—and for the most part, unrelated—areas of the world. Hands off in Europe, the open door plus tough rhetoric in Asia, benevolent dominance in the Western Hemisphere: none of it was necessarily connected; none of it could rely for support or enforcement on anything more than diplomatic notes and undiplomatic but very weak gunboats. The world of international politics, one might argue, did not become one world for the United States until 1942 when war had come in two hemispheres, concurrently, but separately and over different issues. Thereafter the United States had to fight against enemies in the company of allies, to allocate precious resources and military forces in difficult choices concerning priorities of adversaries, geographic regions and objectives, and even of the needs of contending allies.

When the Second World War ended, the problems of decision raised by global war lingered for American policymakers. There remained the strenuous mental exercise of integrating policies and interests in disparate regions of the world into some coherent and analytically useful scheme. And there continued the parallel problem of priorities, of the allocation of money, military equipment, and manpower in a world grown larger and more precarious than most Americans had ever anticipated.

Three factors accounted for the postwar continuation of the political and strategic decision difficulties of wartime. First was the recognition that whatever the ultimate potential might be, America's ready resources for conflict were grossly inadequate to meet all potential requirements amid the confusing hazards of the late 1940s. This disparity between resources and requirements in part was due to the unexpectedly voracious nature of modern war, in which it seemed that men and matériel were consumed at incredible rates; America's small forces in being were simply inadequate for most potential uses. In part the disparity may have been a consequence of over-reliance on the promise for peace of international organization in the first two years following the war, a confidence that proved ill-founded and especially significant for security when the United Nations could not assume responsibility for the control of atomic weapons. In part the inadequacy of ready resources also resulted from the well-known American proclivity for rapid demobilization at war's end, a remnant of traditional and still latent isolationism.

A second reason for the continuation of wartime decision difficulties in policy and strategy developed out of the new ideological unity that characterized postwar problems. From Iceland to Italy, in Asia, and even in Latin America, Communism was showing vigor as a political alternative. In addition it was the professed philosophy of armed opponents to governments supported by the United States in Greece, China, and elsewhere. Ideological categorization emphasized similarities among problems in diverse regions of the world and to a certain extent shaped consistent responses in American policy.

A third reason for the continuation of wartime decision dilemmas—and by far the most important reason as regarded specific aspects of postwar strategy and policy—was the geopolitical position of the Soviet Union. Before the Second World War it had required at least two adversary powers to present the United States with major challenges in East and West. After the war, by virtue of its unique position, the Soviet Union was capable of threatening expansion and harm either in Europe or in Asia. It was even conceivable that Russia's leaders would attempt both simultaneously. More than any other considerations, the fact of Soviet position and the uncertainty surrounding Soviet intentions underlay the new global unity of American postwar foreign policy as it pertained to security and strategy. To the extent that American interests and security could be threatened by events on the European continent, on the Asian mainland, or in the important island groups off Asia and Southeast Asia, the Soviet Union possessed opportunities that could only stimulate American anxiety.

American policymakers of the late 1940s attempted to meet the requirements of globally intertwined security problems by means of an integrated policy and strategy: containment. For the doctrine of containment embodied both a statement of political objective and one of technique, or strategy.[1] The grand objective was to bring about an alteration in the nature of the Soviet system so profound as to change for the better Soviet behavior in international affairs. The technique was first to prevent accretions to Soviet power by employing economic and, if necessary, military measures to forestall Soviet expansionism; and second to weaken Soviet influence beyond Russia's borders by promoting nationalism in the hope of engendering dissidence within the Communist camp. Over time, out of frustration and out of inability to improve its relative power appreciably, the Soviet Union would moderate its aims and methods and become a good international citizen. At that point the United States would have achieved its goal and obviated the greatest part of its postwar security problem.

The author of containment, George F. Kennan, then articulated an idea that was the progenitor of the famous Nixon-Kissinger concept of a pentagonal world; he put that idea at the center of the doctrine. There were, Kennan noted, five areas of the world with far more power potential than any others; these consequently were highly important in the context of competition with the Soviet Union. Only the United States, the United Kingdom, Western Europe (the Rhine Valley), Russia, and Japan had the cultural, physical, and technical resources to become great powers in the modern industrial era. Kennan proposed that, as the heart of containment strategy, the United States and its allies should endeavor to keep four of those five centers free of Soviet control. Kennan and others in policy circles also believed that certain resource-rich areas should be kept out of Soviet hands, principally the Middle East and Latin America.

In terms of strategy, Kennan's idea of containment was neither passive nor reactive, both descriptions that critics have erroneously attached to containment. Instead, it was an active, strategic defense, a form of strategy that maximizes resources and strength and therefore is highly appropriate for long-term application. Europe and Asia, East and West, thus came together not only as problems in American security affairs after the Second World War, but as elements of a common solution in the integrated policy and strategy of containment.

Although Europe and Asia each had a place within a common policy and strategy, containment, their status in that scheme was not identical. The first and most grievous conflicts of interest between the United States and the Soviet Union after the war arose in Europe. That may have been a result in part of the fact that nowhere else in the world did American and Soviet troops and diplomats face each other across invisible political lines, frustrating each other's immediate desires. More fundamental to that situation, however, was the fact that both the Soviet Union and the United States saw in Europe higher stakes, more essential interests, than anywhere else on earth.

In terms of culture, development, skills, resources, and tradition, Europe superseded other regions and so focused the attention of the great powers at war's end. Strategically, it is necessary to note that control of the Rhine Valley had for centuries been the single most important geopolitical determinant of power relationships in Europe. In Europe, from 1944 onward, the Soviet Union expanded and caused crises. To Europe, American policy planners turned first when in 1947 the State Department created its Policy Planning Staff and Congress established the National Security Council. Three of the first four papers from the Policy Planning Staff concerned Europe; the first National Security Council series of memoranda likewise dealt with European problems.

Conclusive demonstrations of American priorities came in the devotion to Europe of Marshall Plan aid—ultimately somewhat more than $13 billion—and correspondingly, military priorities received confirmation in the North Atlantic Treaty of April 4, 1949, the first peacetime military alliance ever signed by the United States.

In Asia the repercussions of these decisions regarding priorities were of enormous consequence. American money would not be going to Asia in like quantity as to Europe, nor would

American military forces in addition to those already deployed to that region. The success of containment policy and strategy in Asia would depend not on infusion of resources as in Europe, but on balancing Soviet opportunities and power via Chinese nationalism, and on reviving Japan by means of a restored regional economy rather than through American aid.

III

At a time when American resources for Far Eastern problems were minimal, the progress of Chinese Communists on the mainland altered power relationships in Asia to an extent that threatened to invalidate current American concepts of regional and global strategy. The military relationship of mainland to islands, the relative power and deployment of Russian and American forces, and even the priorities between Europe and Asia in global strategy came into question.

In the late 1940s the priority of Europe over the Far East imprinted American strategy. In a document of April 29, 1947, the Joint Strategic Survey Committee of the Joint Chiefs of Staff placed the Far East last in terms of regional strategic importance for the United States in the event of war with the Soviet Union and other Communist countries. Western Europe, the Middle East, northwest Africa, and Latin America all ranked ahead of the Far East. In lists of individual countries to which the United States might give military assistance, China stood third from last both in importance to American national security and in a combined estimate of importance and urgency of need. Korea was high in need but very low in importance; it ranked just ahead of China on the same list in the combined estimate.[2]

Europe retained highest priority for two sound reasons of self-interest. First, the United States believed that it would require the support of some of the countries of the "Old World" if it were not to be overpowered by enemies in wartime. Second, in case of war with the Soviet Union and satellite countries, the United States would be most vulnerable in the Atlantic. Unless the United States could count on militarily strong allies on the eastern side of the Atlantic, that ocean might become a "highway" for Soviet attackers.[3] At least, so strategists thought at the time.

This Europe-first logic and correlative priorities soon permeated the strategic guidance of the Joint Chiefs of Staff. Such statements forecast that in war with the Soviet Union, military operations would probably begin in the West and concentrate there. The United States and its allies would have to conduct an urgent, top-priority counteroffensive in Europe and in the Mediterranean. In the Far East, the United States would fight a strategic defensive based on a combined mainland-island position. American strategic planners expected to establish a left flank in Asia extending to and running in part along the Yellow River; they also expected that millions of Nationalist Chinese troops would be available to fight Russian and Chinese Communists. In addition, the United States would have the use of the naval base at Tsingtao in northeastern China. Offshore, the United States would maintain secure air bases, naval bases, and staging areas in Guam, Okinawa, probably the Philippines, and possibly Japan.[4]

The progress of Chinese Communist armies called this entire strategic concept into question. In one indication of the changing strategic context, the National Security Council in May of 1948 began to discuss the withdrawal of American naval units stationed at Tsingtao, near the Gulf of Chihli, because of the increasing danger that they might become involved in joint military operations with Nationalist Chinese naval units against Chinese Communist forces. Such a development would pose a serious political liability in terms of an evolving American plan to lure a Communist China away from too-close relation with the Soviet Union. It would also threaten military embarrassment, for without vast additional resources, military engagement could lead only to defeat and humiliation for American forces in the Far East.[5] Similar considerations of military vulnerability, combined with the aforementioned assessment of Korea as low in importance to American interests, had already resulted in a 1947 decision to withdraw all American forces from that country. Throughout 1948 and 1949 that decision received regular reaffirmation; the withdrawal actually occurred at the end of June 1949.

Well before the American withdrawal from Korea, General Douglas MacArthur, probably the most important individual formulator of American ideas concerning strategy in the Far East, had been devising a strategic concept that might make up in part for dubious position on the mainland. In conversations in March of 1948, MacArthur had explained to George Kennan, the influential director of the Department of State's Policy Planning Staff, that American "strategic boundaries" lay along the eastern shores of Asia, and not, as formerly, the coasts of North and South America. The fundamental strategic task, he said, had become to insure that no serious amphibious force could assemble and venture against American forces or friends from an Asiatic port. The general went on to describe an island air base defense concept for the United States in Asia in terms of an arc in which America needed to maintain striking forces. He sketched a U-shaped area comprising the Aleutians, Midway, the former Japanese-mandated islands, Clark Field in the Philippines, and Okinawa. From these bases, and with adequate air strike forces at Okinawa, MacArthur thought he could prevent projection of amphibious power from the mainland without bases in Japan or Taiwan, although it remained important to keep the strategic facilities of both away from any other power.[6]

Significantly, Kennan not only agreed with MacArthur's formulation, but forwarded the strategic concept to the Secretary of State, George C. Marshall, with slight but meaningful alterations in wording to elucidate the facts and logic of American position in the Far East. His version of the strategic concept had three important points. First, although the United States government would still attempt to "influence events on the mainland of Asia in ways favorable to [American] security, we would not regard any land areas as vital to us. Korea would accordingly be evacuated as soon as possible." Second, "we would rely on Okinawa-based air power, plus our advance naval power, to prevent the assembling and launching [of] any amphibious force from any mainland port in the east-central or northeast [of] Asia." Third, Kennan proposed, "Japan and the Philippines would remain outside this security area, and we would not attempt to keep bases or forces on their territory, *provided* that they remained entirely demilitarized and that no other power made any effort to obtain strategic facilities on them." [7]

The "island air power" strategic concept for the Far East as espoused by MacArthur and Kennan depended on at least two important assumptions not present in their actual strategic concept statements of March 1948. One was an assumption about the timing of contingencies the United States might face in Asia or elsewhere: American strategic planners in the late 1940s assumed that there would be no war with the Soviet Union or its vassals until perhaps 1954. British strategists concurred, and indeed thought the Americans unduly pessimistic; for their estimate was that no serious threats could arise before, say, 1957. Even then, American planners thought, war would more likely result from miscalculation than from deliberate decision.[8] This meant that the United States had considerable time in which to prepare itself; in the longer run, the paucity of resources that had forced postwar decisions on regional priorities might not be so pronounced.

In a second assumption, MacArthur, Kennan, and the Joint Chiefs of Staff were depending on the atomic bomb to make air power effective against attempted offensive operations from the Asian mainland. With the atomic bomb, the American military posture in the Far East could indeed be adapted to the contemporary—and, one hoped, temporary—shortage of resources and to the mission of strategic defensive. An atomic strategy for the region would require a minimum of bases, aircraft, and servicemen. Without the bomb, and in the face of adverse developments in China, such a "minimalist" approach to maintaining a strategic defensive capability in Asia would be out of the question.[9]

Interestingly, the course of the civil war in China in middle and late 1948 brought about significant divergences between Kennan and MacArthur as both attempted to revise their strategic concepts to accord with political and military circumstances. As the situation worsened for the Nationalist armies throughout 1948 and 1949, MacArthur considered the possibility of resisting the course of events, of trying to stave off Nationalist defeat and all that might flow from it. In a long telegram of November 20, 1948, he explained to Army Deputy Chief of Staff General Albert C. Wedemeyer just what had happened to America's military position *vis-à-vis* the Soviet Union as a result of the military successes of the Chinese Communists.[10]

MacArthur assumed that under all circumstances the advances of Chinese Communists would be more beneficial to Russian interests than to American. He also assumed that under certain circumstances Chinese Communists might, and probably would, afford bases and cooperation to the Soviet Union.[11] If Tsingtao fell, he feared, the Soviets would have an opportunity—though not necessarily one they would take immediately—to use naval and air bases in that highly important area. Communist control of China's northern industrial and resource regions would improve Soviet wartime logistic capabilities immeasurably. If Soviet aircraft were to use bases in China, Russian forces would gain the "potential of a double air envelopment of the US Far East perimeter extending from Hokkaido to and including Okinawa." If the Soviets acquired the use of bases as far south as Shanghai, Russian aircraft could menace, and perhaps would attack, not only Japan but Okinawa and the Philippines.

The question of bases was by no means all that troubled MacArthur in the situation. The collapse of Nationalist armies in the north seriously affected American war planning assumptions. There would be no millions of Chinese troops fighting with the United States against the Soviet Union if war should come in the Far East. All the resources that the United States had expected the Soviet Union to commit of necessity against pro-Western Chinese troops in war on the mainland were being freed for direct use against Japan and other supposedly secure American air and naval bases in the Far East Command. Among these resources were an estimated 4,150 combat aircraft the Russians had in the Far East, which raised the possibility that the United States would not be able to acquire the air superiority in that theater on which it had always counted. Chinese Communist forces in passing the Yellow River had already achieved a position that the United States had expected would require 150 days of fighting for the Soviets to reach in war.

MacArthur's conclusion was somewhat understated, given his recital: "It appears that events are overtaking certain other assumptions heretofore used as bases for war planning. It no longer appears realistic to consider the Far East as a static and secure flank in the military contest with communism. . . . the left flank of the strategic outpost line in the Pacific, heretofore considered to be the Yellow River in China, now bends back to the line Okinawa-Guam." In short, the idea of a mainland-island combined defense position would have to be abandoned. So might the even more fundamental assumption of American war planning that the United States would be able to hold in the Far East while conducting strategic counteroffensive warfare in the West.

MacArthur took the occasion of the foregoing analysis to make four further points. First, and this was natural for any theater commander, he emphasized the gravity of continuing reduction of forces allocated to his command. Second, he stressed the increasing importance of Japan in American defense disposition as "the bulwark of the new strategic line"; the maintenance of adequate force in Japan seemed to him requisite for effective military action in the Far East. Third, he criticized the decision of the previous year to withdraw American forces from Korea; the situation seemed to require the indefinite retention in Korea of a token force. Fourth, he raised again the importance of China to the United States as the "fundamental keystone of the Pacific arch," and advocated increased material assistance to Chinese Nationalist forces. MacArthur did not call clearly for the maintenance of a mainland-island defense position; there was a certain—perhaps studied—ambiquity in his position. But he seemed to hope for genuine reconsideration before withdrawing from the mainland. In any case, these were minor inconsistencies in his design.

The general included a resonant appeal for coherent, comprehensive thinking about the problem of China, an appeal that constituted a challenge to "Europe-first" priorities:

> The Chinese problem is part of a global situation which should be considered in its entirety in the orientation of American policy. Fragmentary decisions in disconnected sectors of the world will not bring an integrated solution. The problem insofar as the United States is concerned is an overall one. . . . For if we embark upon a general policy to bulwark the frontier of freedom against the assaults of a political despotism, one major frontier is no less important than another, and a decisive breach of any will inevitably threaten to engulf all. . . . Americas [sic] past lies deeply rooted in the areas across the Atlantic but the hope of American generations of the future . . . lies no less in the happenings and events across the Pacific. . . .[12]

Events in China drove Kennan to conclusions almost opposite from those of MacArthur. The general challenged the Europe-first priority of American policy and strategy; Kennan upheld it. In a reversal of previous attitudes, the general hoped to maintain American troops on the mainland of Asia, in Korea; Kennan recommended accelerated withdrawal. MacArthur and the Joint Chiefs of Staff called for increased aid to the Nationalist Chinese, to "buy time" if nothing else; Kennan thought the price too high, and in any case doubted the "practical possibility of exercising any serious influence on the course of events in China through the extension of further military or economic aid. . . ." [13] For reasons of economy of means as well as of political judgment, Kennan was determined to go with the trends of Asian affairs; in Kennan's view, MacArthur and the Joint Chiefs of Staff were proposing to go against them in costly folly and futility.

In the last months of 1949, and in the first weeks of 1950, it became clear that in policy circles Kennan's judgments had found wider acceptance than MacArthur's. However sound MacArthur's appreciation of the strategic difficulties the United States faced as a result of Chinese Communist advances, his view on the relative importance of America's western and eastern "frontiers" was out of step with conclusions in Washington. No great revision of priorities was in sight. As the general had ruminated on the calamities in his Far Eastern Command throughout 1948 and 1949, the National Security Council and associated bodies had considered how to respond to the critical situation in China. The results of those deliberations came in December of 1949.

In addressing the correlation of containment policy with the realities of Asian affairs, the National Security Council coordinated most of the features of policy and strategy that had evolved over the previous two years of discussion. The overarching objective for the United States was to frustrate Soviet ambition to grow in power. The technique depended principally on the idea of denial: denial of opportunity, denial of unopposed gains, denial of control over areas of the world that might alter significantly the "world correlation of forces."

Within this context of containment, the National Security Council reaffirmed the fundamental military objective for the United States in Asia: successful strategic defense, or holding action, in the event of general war "in order that the major effort may be expended in the 'West.'" Likewise, the NSC restated briefly the island strategy first adumbrated by MacArthur, embraced by Kennan, then clouded over by MacArthur's second thoughts. The United States, one NSC paper read, while avoiding commitment of its military forces, should maintain "a strategic position which will facilitate control of coastal and overseas lines of communication in Asia. . . . This minimum position is considered to consist of at least our present military position in the Asian offshore island chain, and in the event of war its denial to the Communists. . . . The first line of strategic defense should include Japan, the Ryukyus, and the Philippines." [14] The document mentioned repeatedly that in the Far East the United States would have to do without "sizable" forces or resources. In reviewing the political, economic, and military problems facing the United States in Asia at the end of 1949, the National Security Council consistently emphasized not how much the United States would have to do in that region but how little it could do.

IV

Like the civil war in China, conflict in Korea caused consequential alterations in American strategy in the Far East. Much ambiguity about American concepts of security as related to the Far East has stemmed from the unfortunate impression created by Acheson's famous speech to the National Press Club on January 12, 1950. It is now apparent that Acheson was not attempting to define what was "vital" in Asia and what was not, or even what was important to the United States. In the same speech in which he left Korea outside the "defensive perimeter" of the United States, he listed Korea and Japan as Asian nations in which the United States *did* possess a vital interest. Rather than inviting attack, in defining a defensive perimeter Acheson was explaining to the public in general terms the ideas put forward by MacArthur and Kennan and formalized into policy in the National Security Council late in 1949. Acheson was defining not the limits of American interest but the limits of American military resources and capabilities, and he was attempting to do so in a manner not threatening either to the Soviet Union or to Communist China.[15]

The first alterations in American strategy in the Far East occurred when the United States government decided that it would be necessary to respond actively to the North Korean attack. This decision depended for the most part on considerations of the extra-regional significance of the Communist challenge rather than on the intrinsic or local value of Korea to American interests. President Harry S. Truman and Acheson worried about the effects such an incursion might have on the new allies of the United States in Europe. They also thought the attack might mean that the Soviet Union was controlling the Communist governments of Asian nations, perhaps even that of China. It was important, therefore, to meet the attack and to insure that it remained only a probe rather than becoming a first step with the potential for second and third steps threatening to American defense posture on Asia's island periphery. In a crisis meeting at Blair House on the night of June 25, 1950, the Army Chief of Staff, General Omar Bradley, said rather austerely that the United States would have to draw the line somewhere, and the President agreed.[16]

The altered perception of global strategy that underlay the American decision to respond militarily in Korea subsequently received exposition in the middle of 1951. Then the National Security Council carefully noted that the "most immediate threats to US security" lay in Asia rather than in Europe.[17] The NSC did not go so far as to revise previous conclusions about the relative value or importance of the regions in overall American concerns. It was a matter of the moment, not of the design.

Further alterations in American strategy in the Far East resulted from efforts to meet the challenge in Korea in a manner that would not unduly diminish the ability of the United States to protect its more important interests in Europe. For the suspicion of the President and his advisers in June of 1950 was that the action in Korea might be only a Soviet diversion. If the United States overreacted in Asia, it would open great opportunity to the Soviet Union elsewhere. Therefore it was necessary to fight the Korean War with minimum resources, while maintaining and indeed improving American and allied readiness for more widespread war. At the Blair House meeting on June 25, 1950, the President pointed directly to the foregoing concern when he instructed the Departments of State and Defense to estimate where the Soviets would probably strike next. During the conflict in Asia, it was the task of the United

States, as the National Security Council formally noted some months later, "without sacrificing vital interests . . . to avoid precipitating a general war with the USSR, particularly during the current build-up of the military and supporting strength of the United States and its allies to a level of military readiness adequate to support United States foreign policy, to deter further Soviet aggression, and to form the basis for fighting a global war should this prove unavoidable." [18]

The necessity of fighting in Korea while protecting the West and building up military strength led to the virtual destruction of the American strategic concept for the Far East as developed prior to the outbreak of war in Korea; for island-based atomic air power was not yet available in 1950 in quantities sufficient to meet the divergent requirements of West and East. Reluctant to commit American troops at the outset of hostilities, the President asked the Air Force whether it could destroy Soviet air bases in the Far East, if that were necessary. The answer was: "Yes, using atomic bombs." [19] Unfortunately, and despite the importance of atomic air power to postwar American defense, the United States government had not attempted to build up a stock of atomic weapons. Instead, the government had experimented with improvements in bomb design and in production methods. At several points in the late 1940s, there were virtually no bombs at all in the American inventory. When the Korean conflict actually broke out, there were very few weapons ready for assembly.

With atomic bombs in short supply, it seemed unwise to release the few available for use in the Far East and so to leave none, or too few, for potential use in the West. This was particularly true because such weapons were intended for use against significant industrial, population, and military targets of the Soviet Union in the event of general war. American strategists were counting on the bomb somewhat to reduce Soviet war-making capability and morale if general war should come. Such targets were in European Russia, not in the East. The use of atomic bombs on Russian airfields in the Far East would neither cripple nor retard Soviet capability in the West and would therefore constitute an imprudent application of that rare weapon, especially considering that such use might well motivate the Soviet Union to initiate direct hostilities against the United States and its allies. With these factors in mind, it was not difficult for President Truman to accede to the emotional appeals of European leaders, who called on the United States to show moral sensitivity and to abstain from employing its terrible super weapon again in Asia.

The practical inability to use atomic weapons in response to the North Korean attack forced abandonment of the Mac-Arthur-Kennan strategic concept, the island air power idea, and led back to a combined mainland-island posture featuring the employment of conventional land, sea, and air forces. Without the bomb, only conventional response would be possible. If conventional military operations were to be undertaken in northeast Asia, bases in Japan would after all be necessary. If bases in Japan were to be relied upon, it would be necessary to defend the sea lanes to the south, which meant bringing Taiwan more actively into a regional security arrangement. Finally, to ward off future threats to the newly important American position in Japan, as well as to Japan itself, it would be advisable to maintain a military presence on the mainland, in Korea, rather than to leave the mainland once again after having defeated the North Korean invaders. All of the foregoing features of the altered American military posture in the Far East were formalized in treaty commitments between 1951 and 1955. Down to the present writing, in 1977, the United States still remains bound by treaty to defend Taiwan, South Korea, and Japan, this despite the acquisition in the middle 1950s of the atomic capabilities needed, but lacking, for a preferred strategy some five years earlier.

It is interesting to speculate how different the American response to North Korean aggression might have been had the attack come later, more in consonance with the forecasts of strategic planners. The Western Alliance might have been more competent and confident, so that response in Asia would perhaps not have been necessary for reasons of European security. The United States might have developed its atomic capabilities to a point at which it possessed complete assurance that it could prevent offensive operations from the mainland, whatever the local shifts of politics and power in such places as Korea. United States troops would have been out of Korea longer. There would have been time, perhaps, for the Sino-Soviet antagonism to develop more openly, so that American policymakers could have discerned that they had been correct to rely on regional nationalism to delimit Soviet power and opportunity in Asia.

V

It has been common, though perhaps mistaken, to assess the American response to war in Korea as necessary, vigorous, relatively clever in drawing in the United Nations, and effective in terms of the overall objectives of containment. After all, there were no similar tests of Western resolve and capability in Europe; not for many years did another manifestation of Asian Communism pose serious challenge to American interests; Taiwan, Korea, and Japan remained free of Communist domination. It was unfortunate, so analysts have concluded, that in containing Communism in Korea the United States so annoyed the People's Republic of China both by allying with the Chinese on Taiwan and by seeming to threaten China directly with military operations on the mainland. But in most assessments the benefits of the intervention still have seemed to outweigh the costs.

As strategy, however, containment was not only supposed to prevent accretions in Soviet power, but to do so in a manner consistent with the resources available to the United States in the context of global strategy and requirements. Accidents of time and circumstance in China and Korea from 1948 to 1951, and American responses to them, finally increased, rather than decreased, both American security concerns and the resources necessary to manage them in subsequent decades. The American response to aggression in Korea did not decrease the vulnerability of the United States anywhere else in the world, nor even in Asia; it is not even provable that, by example, it deterred similar adventures in later years, for Soviet and Chinese intentions in this regard are impossible to establish. Instead, it seems clear that the American response, and the formalizing of strategic position into security treaties, increased the liabilities of the United States in Asia. This, surely, was no mark of effective strategy.

From the vantage of the 1970s, it is easy to discern the negative consequences of retrogression in American strategy in the Far East from 1948 to 1951. In effect, the strategic posture resulting from the Korean commitment resembled MacArthur's ideas at the time he was having second thoughts, hoping to stave off the loss of usable military position in Asia by means of a revived and revised mainland-island position. The longer range effects, however, validated Kennan's view that to maintain such a position would place the United States in opposition to trends of Asian politics. Operations during the Korean War, and the enlarged American military stance in the Far East afterward, did in fact seem threatening to China. The militarization of American policy in that region also seemed to set the United States against Asian nationalist movements, some of which were Communist. Surely many of the factors elucidated above comprise essential background to the American approach to subsequent problems in Southeast Asia, and especially in Vietnam.

American strategy in the Far East during and after the Korean War obviously made adversaries uneasy; less obviously, over ensuing years, it made friends uneasy. In the aftermath of American involvement in Vietnam—in some respects an unhappy reprise of the Korean conflict—Japan urged the United States to draw down its forces based in Japanese territory, demanded the return of Okinawa, and forced withdrawal of all American tactical nuclear weapons from Japanese soil and naval facilities. As a result of unwanted American military operations during the *Mayaguez* crisis in 1975, another friend,

Thailand, terminated American basing privileges. The strategic position has even made the people of the United States uneasy, so that in recent years there has been a serious reconsideration of American commitments and military deployments in Taiwan and South Korea.

Gradually, and somewhat involuntarily, the United States has had to return to a military posture in the Far East structurally similar to that it intended to establish in the late 1940s. To deter offensive operations outward from Asia, the United States has come to depend on submarine-carried nuclear armaments, functionally equivalent to the strategic air power of the earliest postwar years. For lesser difficulties, the United States has depended recently, as it did in the 1940s and 1950s, on the capability of the Seventh Fleet locally to exert American influence and to perform limited-scale military operations. Perhaps, as Kennan suspected in the 1940s, the United States may find in the 1970s enhanced security in Asia via reduced military involvement.

Notes

[1] John L. Gaddis, "The Strategy of Containment," in Thomas H. Etzold and John Lewis Gaddis, editors, *Containment: Documents on American Policy and Strategy, 1945–1950* (New York, 1978), best presents the features of containment as strategy. See also the Gaddis essay, "Containment: A Reassessment," *Foreign Affairs,* Vol. 55 No. 4 (July 1977), pp. 873–887.

[2] "United States Assistance to Other Countries from the Standpoint of National Security," Report by the Joint Strategic Survey Committee, *Foreign Relations of the United States: 1947,* I, 735–750, esp. pp. 737, 738.

[3] *Ibid.,* p. 739.

[4] See, for instance, JCS 1725 of February 13, 1947, "Strategic Guidance for Industrial Mobilization Planning," and its follow-on paper, JCS 1725/1 of May 1, 1947, in the records of the Joint Chiefs of Staff, Modern Military Records Branch, National Archives, Washington, D.C. David Alan Rosenberg discusses other guidance and early war plans in "The U.S. Navy and the Problem of Oil in a

Future War: The Outline of a Strategic Dilemma, 1945–1950," *Naval War College Review,* XXIX, No. 1 (Summer 1976), 53–64. See also Douglas MacArthur to the Department of the Army, November 20, 1948, *Declassified Documents Quarterly and Reference System,* 75: 258C.

⁵ NSC 11, "Action by U.S. Forces at Tsingtao in Defense of U.S. Lives and Property," May 24, 1948, *Foreign Relations of the United States: 1948,* VIII, 314–316; and NSC 11/2, "U.S. Armed Forces at Tsingtao," December 15, 1958, *ibid.,* pp. 339–342.

⁶ Policy Planning Staff paper 28/2, "Recommendations with Respect to U.S. Policy Toward Japan," containing a memorandum of Kennan's conversations with MacArthur on March 5, 1948, *Foreign Relations of the United States: 1948,* VI, 691–719, esp. pp. 700–702.

⁷ Kennan to Marshall (from Manila), March 14, 1948, *Foreign Relations of the United States: 1948,* I (pt. 2), 531–538.

⁸ JSPC 814/3, "Estimate of Probable Developments in the World Political Situation up to 1957," Report by the Joint Strategic Survey Committee, December 11, 1947, in Etzold and Gaddis, eds., *Containment, op. cit.,* Chapter Six. The difference in British and American views is shown in JIC 429/2, a report of the Joint Intelligence Committee dated August 25, 1948, in the records of the Joint Chiefs of Staff, Modern Military Records Branch, National Archives, Washington, D.C. Kennan consistently at that time, and subsequently, emphasized that the greatest danger of war with the Soviet Union lay in accident, or miscalculation, and not in deliberate intention of the Russians.

⁹ Principal features of early atomic strategy are addressed in the dissertation of David Alan Rosenberg, "Toward Armageddon: Military Professionalism, Interservice Rivalry, and the Foundation of Nuclear Strategy, 1945–1950" (University of Chicago, 1977). See also Chapter Six of *Containment,* Etzold and Gaddis, eds., *op. cit.,* "Implementation: Military Planning, 1947–1950."

¹⁰ MacArthur to Wedemeyer, November 20, 1948, *Declassified Documents Quarterly and Reference System,* 75: 258C.

¹¹ This assumption was pointed out and challenged in a memorandum of conversation by Fayette J. Flexer, Counselor of Embassy in the Philippines, December 7, 1948, *Foreign Relations of the United States: 1949,* IX, 265.

¹² The foregoing quotation comes from a message from MacArthur to Congressman Charles Eaton, March 3, 1948, and was repeated in the telegram to General Wedemeyer of November 20, 1948, as cited above. It has been quoted in numerous monographs and studies.

[13] In the National Security Council, the Joint Chiefs of Staff lobbied strongly for continuing aid to China and attempting to buy time, so that they and MacArthur were in complete agreement. See NSC 22, July 26, 1948, "Possible Courses of Action for the U.S. with Respect to the Critical Situation in China," July 26, 1948, *Foreign Relations of the United States: 1948*, VIII, 118–122; and NSC 22/1 of the same title dated August 6, 1948, *ibid.*, 131–135. For Kennan's views, see Policy Planning Staff papers 39 and 39/1, "U.S. Policy Toward China," dated September 7, 1948, and November 24, 1948, respectively, *ibid.*, 146–165, 208–211.

[14] The discussion of the National Security Council's deliberations late in 1949 in the foregoing paragraphs rests on NSC 48/1, December 23, 1949, and NSC 48/2, December 30, 1949, both entitled "The Position of the U.S. with Respect to Asia," U.S. Department of Defense, *United States-Vietnam Relations, 1945–1967* (Washington, D.C., 1971), VIII, 226–272.

[15] David S. McLellan, *Dean Acheson: The State Department Years* (New York, 1976), pp. 209–17, 267–70. McLellan surprisingly does not make direct use of NSC 48/1 and NSC 48/2 in explaining the immediate background of the Acheson speech.

[16] Ambassador at Large Philip C. Jessup's memorandum of the conversation at the Blair House meeting appears in *Foreign Relations of the United States: 1950*, VII, 157–161. The best brief treatment of Korea's complicated opening issues is John L. Gaddis, "Korea in American Politics, Strategy, and Diplomacy, 1945–1950," in *The Origins of the Cold War in Asia,* edited by Yōnosuke Nagai and Akira Iriye (New York, 1977), pp. 277–298.

[17] NSC 48/3, "U.S. Objectives, Policies and Courses of Action in Asia," April 26, 1952, p. 1, in records of the National Security Council on deposit in the Modern Military Records Branch, National Archives, Washington, D.C.

[18] *Ibid.*, p. 2.

[19] Jessup's memorandum of the conversation at the Blair House meeting, June 25, 1950, *supra cit.*

Readings and Sources

Acheson, Dean G., *The Korean War* (New York, 1971). Acheson's memoirs are unusually useful because he retained and used so much documentation from his years in public service.

——, *Present at the Creation: My Years in the State Depart-

ment (New York, 1969). Acheson's comprehensive memoir to some extent anticipates the more detailed treatment of the Korean question above, but has the value of comprehensive policy context for his years as Secretary of State.

Borg, Dorothy, compiler, *Historians and American Far Eastern Policy* (New York, 1966). This small collection of papers gives much insight into traditional American policy toward China and its explication in American writings of the twentieth century.

Cohen, Warren I., *America's Response to China: An Interpretative History of Sino-American Relations* (New York, 1971). This brief survey of Sino-American relations is a sound beginning for any student.

Etzold, Thomas H., and John Lewis Gaddis, editors, *Containment: Documents on American Policy and Strategy, 1945–1950* (New York, 1978). This volume brings together basic documentation on principal lines of policy and strategy, illustrating the relation between them. It also contains an analytic essay on containment as strategy, as well as one on national security organization and policymaking from 1945 to 1950. The chapter on war planning is especially relevant to the present essay, as is the one on the implementation of containment in the Far East.

Ferrell, Robert H., *George C. Marshall* (New York, 1966), volume XV in the series *American Secretaries of State and Their Diplomacy*, Samuel Flagg Bemis and Robert H. Ferrell, editors. This sensible and sensitive volume remains essential reading for American policy during Marshall's tenure.

Gaddis, John Lewis, "Korea in American Politics, Strategy and Diplomacy: 1945–1950," in *The Origins of the Cold War in Asia*, edited by Yōnosuke Nagai and Akira Iriye (New York, 1977). Prepared as a paper delivered at a conference on "The International Environment in Postwar Asia," Kyoto, Japan, November, 1975, this is one of the first extensive uses of documentation recently declassified and/or published on this topic. It is especially useful for its treatment of great power relations as context for specific developments in Asian strategy and politics.

McLellan, David S., *Dean Acheson: The State Department Years* (New York, 1976). This is the most recent and the best exposition of Acheson's policies and intentions, although it is weak on strategy.

May, Ernest R., *The Truman Administration and China, 1945–1949* (New York, 1975). An essay and documents, this volume argues that the decision on whether or not to aid Chinese Nationalists was considered and reconsidered throughout the late 1940s, and elaborates the stages and terms of that issue.

Paige, Glenn D., *The Korean Decision (June 24–30, 1950)* (New York, 1968). This interesting volume needs to be read in conjunction with Acheson's memoirs and other subsequent works related to the topic.

Schurmann, Franz, *The Logic of World Power: An Inquiry into the Origins, Currents, and Contradictions of World Politics* (New York, 1974). This book is one of the only sustained treatments of the Sino-Soviet-American relationships since World War II. Although the analysis is arguable at many points, it is provocative and worth attention.

Simmons, Robert R., *The Strained Alliance: Peking, Pyongyang, Moscow and the Politics of the Korean Civil War* (New York, 1975). This is the best exposition of the idea that the Soviet Union did not control North Korean behavior and did not order the attack on the South. Interestingly, in contrast to his former views, George Kennan has recently shown some sign of accepting the Simmons argument.

Spanier, John W., *The Truman-MacArthur Controversy and the Korean War* (New York, 1965). The best book on the subject, Spanier's treatment allows glimpses of MacArthur's brilliance as well as his overconfidence.

Tang Tsou, *America's Failure in China, 1941–1950* (Chicago, 1963). Based on thorough use of published sources, including congressional hearings, this large work remains helpful on factual matters but is increasingly questionable in interpretation.

United States Department of Defense, *United States-Vietnam Relations, 1945–1967* (Washington, D.C., 1971). The so-called Pentagon Papers, these twelve volumes are the extended version published for the House Armed Services Committee rather than the abbreviated version based on the papers leaked by Daniel Ellsberg. They contain enduringly important material.

United States Department of State, *Foreign Relations of the United States* (Washington, D.C., various). Produced by the Department of State's Historical Office, these volumes constitute the single most important published source of information and documentation on American policy for the years covered in the series, which at present writing is into 1950.

————, *United States Relations with China, with Special Reference to the Period 1944–1949* (Washington, D.C., 1949). The famous China White Paper contains much documentation that remains of interest.

Chapter Six

America's Relations with China's Leaders: The 1920s to the 1970s

BY JEROME K. HOLLOWAY, JR. AND THOMAS H. ETZOLD

Despite the air of self-congratulation that marked American reaction to President Richard M. Nixon's visit to Peking in February 1972, the grandchildren of today's hand-clasping headmen may consider Ping-Pong diplomacy and its aftermath as one of the most aberrant periods in Sino-American relations. American relations with the leaders of China's sixty-five-year-old revolution have fallen into three periods: first, a learning stage from 1922 until late 1945; second, a hostility period until 1971; and third, the contemporary era that began with the Shanghai communiqué of 1972. In all three phases, fear-filled confusion and ignorance have marked American policy, while self-absorption, rather than self-congratulation, has distinguished Chinese policy.

I

The learning phase in Sino-American relations was long and complicated, and one may wonder whether indeed it has ended—or ever will. From outside China and the United States the paradoxes of Sino-American relations have long been evident. One of the *Times Literary Supplement*'s (*TLS*) then anonymous reviewers wrote about Edgar Snow's book *The Long Revolution,* published in 1972: "Odd, then, that the foreigners with whom he [Mao Tse-tung] should have had the closest contact were Americans, all representatives of the country most anxious to frustrate Mao's nationalist ambitions." In fact, Mao may have had closer contact with either the Russians or the Japanese in his long, sheltered diplomatic life, but it would be difficult to deny that Americans (Snow, John Service, and others) had good rapport with Mao and reported his views with accuracy. Certainly, they never erred so ridiculously as did a young English journalist whose 1933 report described "Mao Dsu Tung, a gifted and fanatical young man of thirty-five suffering from an incurable disease." [1] Still, accuracy of reporting is largely wasted if the readers who matter do not or will not understand it; such reporting becomes worthless when these readers have decided in advance that they are in mortal peril from the subjects of the reporting. These were high among the many failures that set the United States off on eccentric courses toward what would become the People's Republic of China (PRC).

As for China's policy toward America in learning time and beyond, for almost all of the period covered in this essay Mao and his closest advisers probably paid little attention to fulminations in Washington. The immediate aim of the Chinese revolution—the staggering task of integrating and invigorating an impoverished fourth of mankind—left little time for worry whether the United States would allow the Standard Vacuum Oil Company to bunker a British freighter carrying West German fertilizer to Taku Bar on the Gulf of Chihli, the kind of question which in the 1950s and 1960s could convulse large segments of the Washington bureaucracy and roil the relations of North Atlantic allies at Paris or Brussels. Americans have never realized adequately the extent to which the enormous domestic reconstruction of China after 1949 overshadowed external affairs. The aim of revolution was no less than to make a new society from China's traditional order, the millennia-old bases of which had survived alien conquerors, domestic fools and tyrants, and an unforgiving ecological setting. In time Americans may realize the meager concern of Chinese revolutionaries for the problem of adjusting relations with the United States.

Thus analysis of Sino-American relations must begin with the realization that the Chinese long have maintained a priority advocated for the United States in recent years but not attained: internal affairs first, foreign affairs second. Historians who construct from Chinese writings a thesis that "Mao and his colleagues were acutely aware of the need to relate their internal revolution to the world scene" may be able to cite appropriate chapter and verse, but the smell of the lamp hangs over their work; the smell of night soil was both more familiar and more a concern to Chinese leaders.[2] Only the real threat of the Soviet military buildup east of Lake Baikal in the late 1960s brought revision of Chinese priorities; the Chinese attempt to use diplomacy to redress this military problem would, in all likelihood, endure only as long as the problem itself; and that would be the end of foreign policy's recent prominence in China.

Another realization is important for Americans reared on stories of the once-beautiful friendship between the Chinese and American peoples: The malevolence of Communist leadership toward the West and its imperialist face in China was genuine. It was impressed by propaganda on the Chinese people to an extent as yet unmeasurable, but which after a generation is still significant. It has been easy to overestimate just how concerned a Chinese may have been about foreigners. To quote another of the *TLS*'s anonymous reviewers (this time on Wolfgang Franke's *A Century of Chinese Revolution, 1851–1949*), "Most Chinese live out their lives without ever seeing a foreigner . . . one missionary seen in a lifetime was hardly the experience that would awaken more than curiosity. . . ." Chinese propaganda abetted by American political and security paranoia did impress the recognition of this animosity on large numbers of the American people, and the ill feeling was real enough, as noted. However, its verbal, pictorial, and mass expression in China was wildly exaggerated in traditional Chinese fashion, a cultural phenomenon little explained in the United States. Both sides used these outbursts to show that progress was not possible in Sino-American relations. The cynicism of both governments in doing this agitated third countries whose diplomats and intellectuals generally made clear (always, they said, more in sorrow than anger) that the United States should be the more mature. Truth was, the bombast served the Chinese equally well: Peking wanted no accommodation, particularly after the Korean War (or, The Triumphant Defense of the Banks of the Yalu, as Chinese history books may someday call it).

Only one problem of foreign affairs regularly intruded on Chinese leaders' complacent indifference to relations with the United States: Taiwan. Taiwan was the problem in which no Chinese interest could be served by ignoring or reviling the United States. It is easy to list the ways in which Taiwan's existence, secure under an American cloak, was a goad to Peking. American interference stopped the revolution short of glorious completion; in international organizations the United States upheld for years the legitimacy of Taipei over that of Peking; Nationalist Chinese regularly conducted military sorties and sabotage operations from Taiwan against China's coast (always with the cooperation of at least one and usually several American government organizations); and Taiwan's economic success was bitter to watch (Peking never worried overly about Taiwan's political success as "Free China," for Chiang Kai-shek's ways were too well known on the mainland).

Failure to gain control of Taiwan was, of course, no threat to the Communist revolution in China. What did endanger it was the continued existence of an alternative Chinese government, secure from military attack or political subversion because of United States interposition. This government, at least to Peking's mind, was still capable of seizing the revolution. After all, Chiang's Nationalist party, the Kuomintang (KMT), had led and controlled the revolution from 1927 to 1949. The PRC's leaders had no fear that the KMT could return in any of the guises it had worn in those disastrous years, whether nationalism, capitalism, liberalism, or democracy. But in calamity on the mainland—a lost war, a breakaway army in the south, an unappeasable famine, a breakdown of central political control: at such moments Taiwan could be dangerous. No American administration until 1972 pledged itself to restrain Chiang in such circumstances; indeed, such circumstances were anticipated with hope by various American Presidents and Secretaries of State. The KMT might never again lead the revolution, but it could abort it. The threat of an alternative government, for which there were precedents in Chinese history, made Taiwan the foreign policy issue that had to be watched constantly and over which compromise was not possible. There, Sino-American differences were ever present and potentially bloody.

In stressing the primacy of domestic development in the philosophy and operation both of the Chinese Communist Party (CCP) until 1949 and of the PRC thereafter, the intention is not to deny the international experience of either. One must remember that the party was founded in the years when Chinese anti-foreignism rather quickly switched focus from Manchu overlords to what appeared to be Western overlords in the treaty ports, along China's rivers and railways and in China's factories and mines (Mao's first criticism of the United States is said to have been in the May Fourth movement, which arose over the American role in attempts to deny to China former German rights in Shantung province).[3] On the intellectual side, the philosophical basis of anti-imperialism was of foreign origin: Lenin's usefully simple formulation of imperialism as the highest stage of capitalism.[4]

When the CCP came to power its weighty international experience—Soviet treachery in 1927, 1939, 1941, and 1945, Japanese aggression from 1931 to 1945, American mediation and participation in the civil war from 1945 to 1947—was little reflected in the PRC's priorities. These priorities took their order from the harrowing slough into which Chinese society and Chinese political economy had been sliding for over a century.

The PRC wanted international recognition as a general aim in 1949. Once the United States denied this, relations with the Americans could not be very important.

The quarter century of Sino-American tensions, then, rested on the American side on obtuseness and political-security paranoia; on the Chinese side, it depended on old hatreds, on some sense of disdain in the tradition of Sinocentrism, and above all on the threat to the revolution seen in an alternative government standing impregnable in a province of China.

II

In the context of the foregoing generalizations, the quality of the 1949 victors' pre-1945 experience with Americans is worth examining, for the periods of learning and then of hostility in Sino-American relations were closely related. One historian recently referred to early contacts between Americans and Chinese Communists as "a persuading encounter." But Americans' reports of these encounters scarcely persuaded any substantial numbers of their fellow citizens. Changing proportions of indifference, confusion, and ignorance were always present in American perceptions of any facet of China; the Yenan setting of the CCP in opposition, the bandit/warlord terminology, and the differing reports of just what was the ideology of the CCP were all too exotic. Edgar Snow's *Red Star Over China,* in 1935 one of the first important Western books about China's Communists, was read by the general public as romanticism rather than as the expert reporting it was. The few Americans persuaded to a positive view of Chinese Communists acquired their sympathies out of characteristic intellectual and emotional weaknesses. First, their tendency to ethnocentrism was typically American, but it hindered real understanding and approval of Chinese Communists. It was difficult to say of New Life pseudo-Confucians in the Kuomintang, "These people are just like us." Secondly, Americans had a humanitarian bias that favorably contrasted the purposefulness of Yenan with the vicious mess of KMT cities. Finally, these observers had a commitment to democracy (at least in contrast to what they understood to be fascism) so deep that one cannot dismiss it as just another manifestation of ethnocentricity. They thought they saw democracy in Yenan; they knew they did not see it in Nanking or Chungking, the peacetime and wartime capitals of KMT leaders. It is difficult, therefore, to find much serious discussion of Marxism, Leninism, or even imperialism in the two decades of unofficial American exchanges with the CCP.[5]

Official American contacts before 1945 constitute a familiar if infamous ground. The White Paper, the published reports of congressional loyalty and security investigations, the voluminous report of Congress's destruction of the Institute of Pacific Relations, and most recently the autobiographical accounts of some of the harassed and humiliated men who carried on these contacts have left little more to learn.[6] This public record shows that these officials carried out their reporting, analysis, and liaison duties with competence, initiative, energy, and devotion to the best interests of the United States. George F. Kennan did find in their work a certain lack of surefootedness on the higher, slippery slopes of Marxism-Leninism, but never any conscious distortion or disloyalty. From the academic side, Mary C. Wright in reviewing the White Paper in the *Far Eastern Quarterly* early in 1950 concluded that there had been available to the United States government ample accurate information to make sound policy judgments about China after Japan's surrender. That such judgments were not made was because "United States policy toward China is more deeply involved in domestic politics than any other aspect of American foreign affairs." [7] The responsibility for the resultant policy aberrations belongs to the Republican Party of those years, led by its responsible elements as well as by Senators Joseph McCarthy, Harry Cain, William Jenner, William F. Knowland, and others. Many Democrats share this responsibility. Presidents Franklin D. Roosevelt and Harry S. Truman made bad appointments and feckless decisions; President Truman and Secretary of State

Dean G. Acheson overreacted to Republican attacks, particularly upon State Department officers. And, of course, the Democratic side of the Senate had its equivalents of the Republican hatchet men, led by Senator Patrick McCarran.

The Chinese Communist view of the first two decades of intermittent contact with Americans was on two levels. At the person-to-person level the Chinese tried to use these Americans as conduits—unsuccessfully, as noted—but always by stressing the humanitarian and democratic themes so important to the Americans. On the ideological level, however, there was no give-and-take; no matter what some Americans might have inferred, no CCP leader ever left any doubt as to his devotion to Marxist Communism. As General George Catlett Marshall noted with awkward emphasis, they not only so stated that to him, but they also insisted upon it. It is true that on specific issues CCP spokesmen dissembled well. The role of capitalism in the new order, American aid, the rigidity of their program, and the like were often presented in terms intended to be palatable to Americans. The CCP also benefited somewhat from an American reluctance to explore the Yenan view of the world. This was understandable in that neither Yenan nor the CCP played any great international role. It might have helped, for example, if Americans had known that Mao in 1939 thought Neville Chamberlain "the world's Public Enemy No. 1." Then again it might not have meant anything. Yenan's line was the Soviet line in foreign affairs (if not in Chinese affairs). That and anti-Western dogma were enough to insure that in 1945 "the preceding twenty-five years of party teaching could not but limit the range of foreign policy alternatives." [8]

The fashion now is to believe that there were lost opportunities in those years (Mao's wish to visit Washington, for example). Yet, the Soviet Union, much closer to the problem and directly involved, chose to accept the legitimacy of Chiang's government over the CCP's claims and interests by signing a treaty with him in August 1945. The CCP accepted that defeat (a Communist leader explained the treaty to the cadres with plaintive understatement: "Soviet policy cannot be understood") and chose to carry on the fight.[9]

Even if the United States had seen the truth of John Davies' analysis that the future of China belonged to the Communists, not Chiang, there never was a way for the United States to drop its support of one of the nominally major members of the victorious United Nations.[10] In something of a paradox, to prop up that ally by large military action on the Chinese mainland was beyond either American power or will in the aftermath of World War II. The United States was stuck.

What it could do and did try was to help the KMT and CCP form a coalition, though always with the aim that the KMT would be the major party. Americans in China, both official and unofficial, had been trying to report to their government and to their readers that the KMT had neither the power nor the general support to be the senior partner. The Communists were trying to tell both America and the world that the United States could not be evenhanded when the aim was to retain the KMT as the senior partner, and that with the substantial military and economic assistance the United States was giving the Nationalists, American mediation was badly compromised. The miscarrying of the mediation seems in retrospect to have been inevitable given this contradiction. Not inevitable, however, was the disastrous American domestic division that accompanied and followed this failure.

III

The hostility period began November 27, 1945. On that day Ambassador Patrick Hurley resigned. His view of the China mediation process as of July 1945 soon appeared in the White Paper in 1949:

> The leadership of the Communist Party is intelligent. When the handwriting is on the wall [when they see that the Soviet Union

is backing the KMT], they will be able to read. . . . The strength of the armed forces of the Chinese Communists has been exaggerated. The area of territory controlled by the Communists has been exaggerated. The number of Chinese people who adhere to the Chinese Communist Party has been exaggerated. State Department officials, Army officials, newspaper and radio publicity have in a large measure accepted the strength of the Communist Party in China. Nevertheless with the support of the Soviet the Chinese Communists could bring about civil war in China. Without the support of the Soviet the Chinese Communist Party will eventually participate as a political party in the National Government.[11]

In November 1945, as Hurley saw the failure of this conception, he blamed the professionals on his staff for supporting the Chinese Communists and complained: "We are permitting ourselves to be sucked into a power bloc on the side of colonial imperialism [defined as Dutch, English, and French] against Communist imperialism." None of this made much sense except to the egregious Hurley, particularly when he claimed in the same tirade that the Soviet Union was not backing the CCP. Hurley's failure to reconcile the KMT and the CCP nevertheless had large consequences. His resentment as expressed in writing and conversation ("the mother ——, he tricked me!" was his ultimate comment on his negotiations with Mao) had much to do with the beginnings of the witch-hunt for those who "lost China." [12] This, it must be said, was a monumental accomplishment for a man of so little talent.

Hurley's failure to reconcile the KMT and the CCP also set in motion the 1946 mission of General Marshall, a yearlong odyssey that made irreversible impressions on the man who would next become Secretary of State. As soon as Hurley resigned, Truman appointed Marshall to go to China, apparently at the suggestion of the Secretary of Agriculture.

The failure of Marshall's effort in China—he sought the same coalition of KMT and CCP as had Hurley—had a history of its own. Two strains ran melancholy courses through the mission. First, suspicion and ill will (both terms, perhaps, too mild) on both sides made compromise unlikely; too much blood and too many treacheries had been invested by both sides in behalf of their totalitarian ways. The second strain was the consistent KMT exploitation of the flaw in the American mediation. KMT policy was to use American assistance to the utmost to seek military victory, while Marshall and the CCP were kept in play in the mediation process. Repeatedly, at Changchun, Kalgan, and in Manchuria and Shantung generally, the KMT sought decision by arms against both the wishes and the advice of the United States government. The KMT was convinced that the United States had no choice but to support the Nationalists; the Communists for their part could not help but see the United States as playing a double game, although as Marshall noted in his final report, they themselves did "not hesitate at the most drastic measures to gain their ends."

Mediation ended in some confusion officially on January 29, 1947. Wang Ping-nan, secretary of the CCP mediation team, commented: "The only way out is to fight." The KMT response to the end of mediation was a new offensive in Shantung on February 2, 1947, using 500,000 troops. On February 15 in a Chinese version of *chutzpah*, Chiang Kai-shek blamed the United States for prolonging the war because it had held up arms and credits several times during the mediation process in futile attempts to restrain the KMT drive for military victory.

American policy confusion continued after the end of the mediation. As the People's Liberation Army (PLA) started to hack at the overextended Nationalists in Manchuria, the Nationalists on June 20, 1947, appealed for more aid from the United States. The American response on June 27 was to announce the sale of ammunition valued at $6.5 million. Then, on July 2, the new Secretary of State, Marshall, explained that these sales did not signify United States support for Nanking. It was all rather difficult to keep straight.

President Truman once more moved tentatively toward further American involvement with the mission of General Albert C. Wedemeyer late in the summer of 1947. The American Embassy reported that the Communists were "vituperative of the Mission" and "generally suspicious and critical" of the Mission's objectives. The Nationalist reaction was that "Wedemeyer paid more attention to the people outside the government than in it" and that the government would change no domestic or foreign policies because of Wedemeyer's observations. Truman then managed to engage the further suspicion and vituperation of the China Lobby by suppressing Wedemeyer's final report for about two years.

As the United States continued ensnared in the China situation, rot set in at Nanking and in its armies, the CCP became more and more angry and contemptuous of American policy, and the Nationalists decided to play for a Republican victory in the 1948 presidential election and for the full support they thought would then be forthcoming. In another domestic development, the United States government suffered a certain loss of control of the foreign affairs apparatus. State, Defense, and the Central Intelligence Agency, still new to the National Security Council harness, were not pulling quite in unison during the KMT debacle. American policies consequently were mixed: some ingenuous, some ingenious, some redolent of the old days of the treaty ports, and some just confused.

In the confusion, however, there was consistency in the basic policy of nonintervention, a consistency insured by the Democratic victory in the 1948 election. The embassy at Nanking waited a decent seventy-two hours after Governor Thomas Dewey's defeat to tell Washington that "short of actual employment of U.S. troops no amount of military assistance could save present situation . . . there was no military step China or the U.S. could take in sufficient time to retrieve the military situation." [13] With his hoped-for Republican victory foreclosed, Chiang waited until December to sound out the embassy on his possible withdrawal from active control of the government; the consul general at Shanghai had been approached on November 29. Even in this matter American authorities gave only guarded answers. The United States wanted no responsibility for any last-minute Nationalist maneuvers.

No matter how deftly Truman and Acheson avoided what looked like a deathbed embrace from the KMT, they never had any possibility of meeting the new Communist regime in China even halfway. Their problem had several parts. First was the fear—a conviction of many Americans—that China would just be an Asian ancillary to the Soviet threat then unfolding in Western Europe. Next, the intense and almost hysterical pressure of the Republicans and some Democrats over "the loss of China" and the Hurley-inspired witch-hunt in the State Department paralyzed American officials. Then, there was at the top of the administration a cultural lag that would not let it see Asians, particularly Communist Asians, as international equals. This last view was shared by many Americans in China.

A cursory rundown of the policies actually followed shows the result of Washington's inability to handle these obstacles to working relations with the CCP.

Economic Aid as a Substitute   In November 1947, in a move to appease its domestic critics, the administration asked for a new China economic aid program of $300 million to begin in April 1948. Secretary Marshall admitted that there was difficulty finding places where the aid might have even a "70 percent possibility of effective use." The Nationalists called the program a "drop in the bucket" and asked for $3 billion over three years. Truman raised the request to $570 million in February 1948, at which time the Republicans criticized the lack of any military aid. Eventually, Congress approved $463 million, which included $125 million to be spent as the Chinese government wished. This was the time when Americans in Nanking were singing a verse to the tune of "O Tannenbaum":

Kuomintang, O Kuomintang,
Always right and never wrong.
Victory after victory mounts
In growing Zurich bank accounts.

Marshall's pessimism was justified. When the PLA captured Tientsin, Shanghai, and other cities, they found warehouses full of United States- and United Nations-supplied aid—cotton, rice, textiles, and more. After a pretense at negotiation for an orderly turnover of these stocks, the new authorities seized them. American losses, if that is the term, were in the millions.

Continuation of United States Military Advice   An American military advisory group was in China from 1946 onward. Throughout the civil war it gave almost daily operational advice to the Nationalist Ministry of Defense, advice rarely taken. As late as December 1948, American officers were urging speed for an all-out attack by nine Nationalist armies south of Hsuekow; the attack did not come off. The advisory group was recalled soon after this because its members had no diplomatic immunity and could have been treated as prisoners of war or mercenaries by the PLA.

United States Marines' Defense of Tsingtao   The United States Navy installation at Tsingtao as of January 1948 had "no formal written agreement" with the Chinese, but was operating because the American fleet commander "considers he has the Generalissimo's personal concurrence in the use of China's ports and waters." [14] Naval officers at Tsingtao told the consul general there that they "were not certain why the Navy was there"; the consul general's explanation was partly "an old tradition of a United States Navy summer training establishment in North China, partly because the die-hards in the Navy hate to give up their hold on this strategic harbor." The Navy was prepared to defend the city and its suburbs alongside the Nationalists with 3,600 Marines and 16 fighter aircraft. The Joint Chiefs of Staff approved the defense in May 1948. After State Department appeals, the National Security Council modified this to "wide discretionary authority" in October 1948, but President Truman took a position that "withdrawal from Tsingtao [was] not to take place at this time, and that aid to North China [was] to be expedited." The State Department was reduced to asking its consul general for reports for "confidential use" as to how the Navy was using its authority. In any event, the Navy evacuated Tsingtao before its capture.

Attempt to Detach Formosa   The National Security Council, fearful both of Nationalist and of Communist use of Formosa, ordered attempts to see (a) whether a local non-Communist government could be set up to give the island "at least a modicum of decent government"; (b) whether the influx of mainland Chinese to the island could be stopped; and (c) whether discreet contact could be made with a Formosa autonomy movement should it serve United States national interests. This was on February 3, 1949; on February 8 the consul general at Taipei (unaware of the National Security Council order) telegraphed Washington: "Evidence increasing Gimo's [Generalissimo Chiang Kai-shek] hand operating here." Chiang had shipped the government's gold and silver reserves to Formosa when he "retired" from the presidency in January 1949. He had also begun diverting United States aid vessels to Formosa and, perhaps equally important to Chinese, he had shipped to Formosa the imperial art treasury, China's heritage of the dynasties from the Han onward. The State Department detached a senior officer from Nanking to explore on the spot the chances for carrying out the National Security Council's policy directives. His report in May 1949 said that any opportunities to keep Formosa out of either Communist or Nationalist hands had passed; the KMT was secure for the moment in its island refuge. The possibility of United States support for a Formosan autonomy movement, never very likely of success, was alive until the Shanghai communiqué of 1972. Even so, Peking did not lose its suspicion about an American role in a separatist movement.

Aid to Nationalist Blockade   After the fall of Shanghai the Nationalist government issued an order "closing" that port and others to all shipping. An American note in June 1949 said that "in the absence of a declaration and maintenance of an effective blockade" the United States would not recognize the order. American vessels of the Isbrandtsen Line chose to risk the run to Shanghai, whereupon Secretary Acheson encouraged the Hydrographic Office to designate the waters around Shanghai "dangerous," thus putting the shipmaster who used those waters at risk of a Coast Guard hearing for loss of his license. Isbrandtsen persisted, and Acheson and the shipping line began a nasty newspaper fight. More important, Chinese Nationalist warships (all vessels received in American military aid) fired on the freighters and holed some of them while United States naval vessels on station off Shanghai looked on.[15] When the Shanghai consular corps complained of the hardship the port closure was causing the city's foreign residents, the State Department wired its consul general: "Established policy this Govt take no action which would have effect lessening effectiveness Nationalist 'blockade.' . . ." The "blockade" ended effectively when Soviet fighter planes appeared over Shanghai in February 1950 to protect the city from Nationalist B-24 Liberator air raids from Formosa. Madame Chiang had told a visiting British businessman in Taipei ("with tears in her eyes," he reported) that Shanghai would have to be destroyed. The "blockade" was revived as a nuisance for a time during the Korean War.

Economic Sanctions on the New Regime The persistent American belief in governmental economic pressures as a political weapon influenced policy early on against the Communists. In 1949 Washington sounded out its European allies on control of mainland trade in strategic goods. In 1949–1950 there were recommendations to stop consular invoice services for Communist state trading companies. The disruption occasioned by war had left large stocks of tung oil, feathers, hog bristles, human hair, and tungsten ready for shipment. The Communists, however, bypassed the consulates as soon as they discovered that American banks would pay letters of credit against shipping documents alone. This development contributed to the demise of the consular invoice system a few years later.

Keeping a Consular Presence Washington had decided in the fall of 1948 to maintain consular posts on the mainland, while the embassy followed the retreating government to Canton and later to Taipei. The stripped-down offices were to be listening posts and possibly the means of opening relations with the victors. No opening came, and it was the fault of both sides. The new authorities did not recognize the consulates and forced officers to sign even the most routine document as "ex-vice consul" or "ex-consul." The Americans refused to do or to ratify any act that might be construed as some recognition of the new regime. This ploy, possible in consular practice because consuls, unlike diplomatic officers, are not accredited to a national government but to a specific provincial area, worked for the British for twenty years at Tamsui on Formosa, but failed in American usage. Two American consular officers were mistreated by the Communists, although in both cases it never became clear that the officials had behaved with discretion. The consular offices were allowed to keep their direct radio contact with Washington and in general were not molested. In February 1950 the municipal authorities at Peking requisitioned parts of the American, British, Dutch, and French consular offices, which had been military barracks for foreign troops stationed at Peking after the Boxer treaties. The other countries accepted the requisition order; the United States did not, using as a counterthreat the withdrawal of all American consular officers. This threat may seem a worrisome commentary on the sophistication of American diplomatic tactics, but truth was that there was no political will for accommodation on either side. American domestic feelings did not permit compromise, and the Chinese, as they showed in the case of the more accommodating British, were interested in settling old scores, which later brought anguish to many innocent Americans living in China.

The White Paper Backfire   The publication of the White Paper in August 1949 was a failure on all sides, except perhaps that of the diplomatic historian (and even he did not get the full record; such things as the Formosa detachment caper were left out). The publication set forth the iniquities of the Nationalists in detail at a time in their fortunes that made the ignominy gratuitous. It did nothing to appease domestic critics, for the few who read it did not believe it. And it proved a boon to Communist propaganda. The White Paper not only documented the flaw of the mediation effort and the anomalies of the nonintervention policy but, in the covering, published transmittal letter, Acheson showed Mao that the best Americans would condescend to offer would be their "traditional support for the Open Door." [16] Mao's reply was savage:

When the People's Liberation Army crossed the Yangtze River, the U.S. colonial government at Nanking fled helter-skelter. Yet His Excellency Ambassador Stuart sat tight, watching wide-eyed, hoping to set up a shop under a new signboard and to reap some profit. . . . In short, he was left out in the cold, 'standing all alone, body and shadow comforting each other.' There was nothing left for him to do, and he had to take to the road, his briefcase under his arm . . . Leighton Stuart has departed and the White Paper has arrived. Very good. Very good. Both events are worth celebrating.

Although the White Paper and later publications illustrated the confusion of American policies, they left Mao scornful of American goodwill; there was nothing from the Chinese side on which any relationship could have been built. A French observer has written:

> With the failure of the Marshall mission and the beginning of the cold war in the West, the [Chinese] tone became one of unprecedented violence. The communists shamelessly falsified obvious historical facts, attributing the defeat of Japan to the Soviet Union's entry into the war, for instance, and tirelessly slandering the United States, accused of wanting to enslave or colonize China. Appearances were in their favour; it was easy for them to show up disinterested gestures, such as economic and military aid, handing over surplus materials, and completely unexceptional treaties . . . from the angle best suited to their own purposes. Minor incidents were violently exploited and many more created.[17]

IV

With the Korean War, Sino-American relations passed into a second phase of the long period of hostility. As the policies outlined above imply, before 1950 the PRC had merely been the winner in a war of concern to the United States, but not one vital to its interests. After 1950, active opposition to the PRC assumed much greater prominence in American policy. The tragedy of the Korean War was that it came unbidden either by China or by the United States. It was truly Stalin's last masterpiece of deceit and violence toward both allies and enemies, perhaps unwitting, but conclusive as a foil to any American hope of exploiting a Sino-Soviet split. The war, whatever its still somewhat obscure origins in Soviet-North Korean relations, hardened the distorted mold of Sino-American relations until the Nixon trip to China some twenty years later.

The overall results of the Korean War now seem fairly clear. China was recognized as a *de facto* great power, most importantly by the United States, and by itself started to assume *de facto* leadership of the Third World. The United States went to a strategic defensive in East Asia based on Taiwan and involving other offshore and peripheral positions. Most important, the United States began to rest Pacific policy on the political, military, economic, and cultural containment of China, while awaiting the overthrow of China's government. In working out this overall set there were cycles of aggression and passivity on both sides. Today American memories, official and public, are confused about the content and sequence of the various crises that came into each cycle. Chinese official memories are probably not so dim and, as previously noted, Westerners really know little about the Chinese citizenry's view of that era or the United States.[18]

Of course Taiwan remained at the center of the Washington-Peking relationship. The Chinese intervention in Korea was not a political interposition to save North Korea or to extend China's influence. It was a reaction to a military threat to China's security. Once that violent episode was over, with no winner save possibly Moscow, the Chinese found the Taiwan question basically altered (American terminology for the island changed about this time because it was thought the use of a Chinese name for the province would enhance Chiang's claim to stand for all of China). Truman had made clear in January 1950 that the United States policy of nonintervention in the civil war applied to Taiwan. American interposition came in June with the Korean War, and a secret policy change to quasi-intervention in 1951 received public emphasis in 1953 when President Eisenhower "unleashed" Chiang Kai-shek to attack the mainland. He was "released" in December 1954 as part of the American mutual security treaty with Taiwan, a leashing never completely effective because in the American military and intelligence agencies Chiang quickly found allies who would support his raids on the coast with or without ambassadorial or presidential approval. These were mere pinpricks to the PRC, but they underlined that American intervention had made China impotent in the Taiwan Strait.

The series of Taiwan crises that took place in the 1950s and 1960s were brought on by China's attempts to overcome its impotence. China could bring pressure against the United States by alleging that "threats to the peace" were arising from a Taiwan crisis. At such times the Soviet Union might see its interest in a Communist victory over Taiwan or, alternatively, it might be blackmailed into fraternal support. The KMT might be bluffed or frightened into some form of accommodation. Finally, international pressure might end the "threat to peace" by forcing the negotiation of a peaceful mainland take-over. None of these possibilities developed into actuality. When candidates John F. Kennedy and Richard M. Nixon debated the subsidiary issue of Quemoy-Matsu before the election of 1960, Kennedy discovered that any compromise on Taiwan or the offshore islands would result in revival of the "loss of China" issue to damage the Democrats. His administration's subsequent failure to ease Sino-American tensions related in part to this perception, although the growing Vietnam problem seemed to leave no room for initiative.

In studying the recurrent crises in the Strait, J. H. Kalicki found that they ended not in solution attained through conference, negotiation, or successful crisis management, but through confrontation on the spot.[19] Neither side wanted general war; that was all on which they could agree; and so mutual, temporary withdrawals became substitutes for solutions. The main issue, Taiwan, remained and festered well beyond the new era opened in 1971–1972.

Americans and mainland Chinese also confronted each other

over events in Indochina, a fact about which there hangs an air of unreality in the late 1970s. Less than a decade before the new era, Secretary of State Dean Rusk was matching invective with Chinese propagandists, the Americans invoking fears of "yellow peril," the Chinese poking fun at a "paper dragon" and at the "freaks and monsters" whom President Lyndon B. Johnson sent abroad as diplomats. Until the Vietnam intervention took on a life (or a death wish) of its own, the United States professed to see the war as a test of Chinese and American wills. In the final days of the French defeat the National Security Council was prepared to blockade China, with no hesitation over the fact that blockade was an act of war.[20] The possible parallels to Korea were always present in American deliberations over action in Vietnam, but as in Korea care over the possibility of a Soviet intervention was marked. The eventual "solution" of the war and the future of the successor states lay in what became unilateral American withdrawal after years of constant failure to engage either the PRC or the Soviet Union in a peace effort.

During these crises of the 1950s and 1960s formal Sino-American contact continued fitfully through ambassadorial-level talks begun as part of the Geneva settlement of 1954. These talks produced one agreement on exchange of personnel. However, for propaganda abroad and at home the mechanism of the talks always seemed more important to the United States than the results. Much of the academic-foundation-media community had become increasingly critical of the futility of American policy toward Peking. By pointing to these talks and later, of course, to the Vietnam war, the United States held off its critics and gave life support to the bureaucratic machinery built up to contain and isolate China.

Many Washington departments had large segments that depended for existence on anti-China policy. The State Department's "China enforcers" had lives of their own, usually distinct from the main lines of American foreign policy. In any showdown over China policy they could be confident of winning because Secretaries of State Dean Acheson, John Foster Dulles,

Christian Herter, and Dean Rusk were never going to open themselves to a charge of softness on China. In the Treasury Department, the Foreign Assets Control group had a zealot's devotion to China policy. Until Fidel Castro came along, it was their *raison d'être*. In addition, they had discovered that no China control position could be too absurd not to win backing on Capitol Hill (one example: not to allow Americans living in Hong Kong to buy fresh food because 92 percent of the colony's fresh food came from China). The Department of Commerce had an elaborate export control mechanism that would be brought ponderously into action to prevent Parker 51 pens, condoms, and sunglasses from reaching China. The Defense Department and the Joint Chiefs of Staff had the largest numbers of China watchers and China controllers. The Pentagon was always willing to run military risks against China that were unthinkable against the Soviet Union. The more than five hundred protests of American air and sea violations of China's frontiers were not all Peking propaganda. For the Central Intelligence Agency's covert side (its overt side was both realistic and restrained over China) the mainland presented a fine field for fun and games, limited only by the regrettable but unchangeable fact that white skin and round eyes were overly visible on Shanghai sidewalks. The United States Information Agency (as well as the CIA) spent millions of dollars on anti-Chinese propaganda; many reputable scholars still unwittingly fill their China bibliographies with USIA-CIA books. And much of the literature of bureaucratic politics flowing from political scientists had its origins in observation of Washington's China hands.

In the Third World also the United States saw itself competing with Peking. Chinese failures and excesses, as well as the individuality of many of the states of the Third World, dimmed Third World admiration for things Chinese, except when the Chinese managed to score off the West or to produce a nuclear explosion or exportable surpluses. Nevertheless, Washington continued to believe it had a duty (and a chance) to contain Peking in the Third World, even while that world was rejecting the American model as applicable to its societies.

Sterility of American policy and vituperation of Chinese policy ("Peking's behavior is violent, irascible, unyielding and hostile," Dean Rusk told the Senate in 1966) halted at least temporarily with the Nixon breakthrough of 1971. The Sino-Soviet dispute, its existence long denied by the United States, gave both Peking and Washington a chance to end the post-1945 era of hostility. It was as if scales dropped from many eyes, and great—though premature—was the rejoicing thereover.

V

With the visit of President Nixon to Peking in February of 1972, Sino-American relations entered a new phase. The visit was, as the President remarked in one of his favorite adjectives, a "historic" mission. Nixon went to Peking without illusions, realizing that "twenty years of hostility could not be swept away in one week of talks." That was realistic. He went in search of peace. That was less realistic. He went imbued with a sense of greatness. After all, before his trip no less a statesman than Premier Chou En-lai had said that the Americans were a great people; Nixon in return generously acknowledged that the Chinese were great too. That was fatuous, and it brought to mind one of the remarks of a turn-of-the-century cartoon character, Mr. Dooley, the Irish barkeep created by Finley Peter Dunne. At the time of the Spanish-American War, Dunne had reported a conversation in Dooley's saloon: " 'We're a gr-reat people,' said Mr. Hennessey earnestly. 'We ar-re,' said Mr. Dooley, 'We ar-re that. An' the best iv it is, we know we ar-re.' "

The theme of the Nixon visit, the goal of the quest as expressed by both Chinese and American leaders, was to discover whether the United States and China could have differences without being enemies. At a time when the United States remained peripheral to the Chinese revolution, when Chinese official malevolence still had deep roots, and nothing really had been done about Taiwan, that was no small order. And with only a few years' retrospect, it is extremely difficult to discern to what extent that order may have been filled, for ambiguities—some deliberate, some inadvertent—surrounded almost every feature of the visit, including the joint communiqué issued at its close.

The gaping disjuncture between words and accomplishments in the Nixon visit to China created an almost surreal atmosphere, an air of paradox: Westerners disoriented in the Orient; great leaders and small deeds; the profound and the banal tumbling over one another. There was Nixon praising the magnificence of the dinner in the Great Hall of the People while trying not to cough after drinking *mau-tai,* the potent grain liquor favored among Chinese but harsh to Western palates. In fact, the Chinese had carefully understaged the Nixon visit: small crowds, only a five-course dinner (Chinese everywhere noted this, for elaborate Chinese dinners can run to twenty or more courses), and no extravagant publicity.[21] Nixon was kept in his place and this served to underline, first for the Soviet Union and second for the rest of Asia, the magnitude of the Chinese triumph. The President of the United States had come to talk largely on Peking's terms. The Soviet Union's freedom of action with regard to China had diminished. China's self-imposed diplomatic isolation of the Cultural Revolution had ended. Chiang Kai-shek had been put on notice. Japan had to face a difficult choice between continued alliance with the uncertain and unceremonious Americans and neutrality with Chinese friendship.

Disturbingly, the American President, his advisers, and his fellow citizens seemed to remain oblivious to the many signs and portents of the visit. American television brought the great banquet to the homes of millions of Americans, scarcely any of whom realized that they were watching their President's abasement. The pedestrian intellect of the President, so strikingly evident in the transcripts of White House tapes published later in the course of the Watergate proceedings, appeared from time to time in the visit. The President visited the Great Wall of

China, and there he told members of the press that it was indeed a great wall and that it must have been built by a great people with a great past and a great future. Nixon then said, "It is worth coming sixteen thousand miles just to stand here to see the wall. Do you agree, Mr. Secretary?" And the Secretary of State, William Rogers, replied: "I certainly do, Mr. President. It is really a tremendous privilege we have had." The President continued: "Let me ask the members of the press, do you think it was worth coming?" Reporters: "Yes, Mr. President." It was a saddening litany.

Amid the banquets, travels, and sight-seeing, President Nixon and his retinue took time out at several moments for "plenary sessions," that is, discussions with Chou En-lai, one rather brief meeting with Chairman Mao Tse-tung, and talks with other officials. At trip's end, the results of these discussions and of preliminary conversations among underlings appeared in a joint communiqué. Issued at Shanghai on February 27, 1972, the communiqué was supposed to become the fundamental document, the bench mark, for a new era of constructive though gradual improvement in relations between America and China.[22]

The air of the surreal—of paradox or what the good Chinese Marxists would call contradictions—carried over into the Shanghai communiqué, for it was a curious blend of three ingredients: one part cautious diplomatic prose, one part stirring revolutionary rhetoric, and one part lie.

The first ingredient, caution, marked the opening paragraphs of the communiqué. The leaders of the two countries, so they themselves said, "found it beneficial to have this opportunity, after so many years without contact, to present candidly to one another their views. . . ." Because representatives of both sides recognized that the most important differences between China and the United States were beyond resolution at that time, the first portion of the communiqué contained general statements of policy for the two countries along with specific points of view on matters in which both Chinese and Americans had interests. The statement was full of pieties: The United States was for justice and freedom, against tension and war, and concerned for the common good. The Chinese pieties, variations on a revolutionary theme, included opposition to bullying, intervention, and power politics, resistance to oppression and support for revolution and liberation.

In specifics, Americans and Chinese attempted to show their ability to agree to disagree. The United States endorsed self-determination for the peoples of South Asia and so did the Chinese; each meant to indicate support for opposing sides in the Vietnamese war. The United States affirmed its commitment to South Korea; China expressed its hope for peaceful unification of Korea on the basis suggested by the Communist government in the North. The United States emphasized the high value of its friendly, close bonds with Japan; China stressed its opposition to the revival of Japanese militarism and its interest in helping the Japanese people build a democratic, peaceful, and neutral Japan. In a last point, the United States took the side of India in the Kashmir dispute in Central Asia; China strongly endorsed the side of Pakistan.

The second ingredient of the Shanghai communiqué, the revolutionary rhetoric, was dispersed as regards location in the document, and some portions were almost concealed and really not so stirring. The Chinese had prefaced their policy pieties and positions with high-flying language about oppression and resistance, liberation and revolution, the latter of which, they asserted, had become the "irresistible trend of history."

Most noteworthy, however, was the inclusion of some principles of international relations on which the United States and China agreed as a basis for mutual relations: "respect for the sovereignty and territorial integrity of all states, nonaggression against other states, noninterference in the internal affairs of other states, equality and mutual benefit, and peaceful coexistence." These fine-sounding principles were none other than the Five Principles of Peaceful Coexistence enunciated by China in 1954 when it first made a serious bid for leadership of the Third World. Enshrined in the proceedings of the Bandung conference of 1955, the principles had been tried briefly, in 1963, in Sino-Indian relations also. There is no indication that anyone in the American delegation paused to reflect on the peculiar fate of that fleeting friendship. There was, however, a moment of embarrassment for Henry A. Kissinger, the chief American architect of the document. One reporter attached to the official party asked upon the communiqué's appearance: "Is this the first time that a President of the United States has formally picked up the language of the Five Principles of Peaceful Coexistence?" Kissinger was not sure, and hastened to add that it did not matter who had put forward the proposals, but it was a lame answer.

Two other topics received significant attention in the communiqué, Taiwan directly and the Sino-Soviet-American relation indirectly; and here the third ingredient, lies—or at best half-truths—came into view. The section on Taiwan was the technical high point of the communiqué, "the crucial question" as the Chinese called it. China directly challenged the United States-Taiwan political and security relationship: "The liberation of Taiwan is China's internal affair in which no other country has the right to interfere." The United States position was the well-known formulation that "All Chinese on either side of the Taiwan Strait maintain there is but one China and that Taiwan is a part of China." Americans clearly had lost sight of the fact that the statement was not true. The United States did not mention its relation with the Taiwan government, but agreed that the final settlement of the Taiwan issue should be left to the Chinese themselves. There was one serious implied challenge to the Chinese position; the United States agreed only to reduce its forces on Taiwan as "tension in the area diminishes."

Direct attention to the Sino-Soviet-American relation was nearly as important as the Taiwan issue in its overall implications, and was similarly riddled with half-truths. At one point in the communiqué the representatives of the two countries agreed on this language: "Both sides are of the view that it would be against the interests of the peoples of the world for any major country to collude with another against other countries, or for major countries to divide up the world into spheres of interest." This was supposed to mean that neither country was "aiming" at the Soviet Union in its quest for improved Sino-American relations, but in fact both were doing exactly that.

The concluding sections of the communiqué covered exchanges, trade, and provisions for further "concrete consultations" to be made by American high-level visitors to China.

One cannot gainsay the American gains, as distinct from Nixon's political gains. An expensive and illogical American policy had been liquidated. The United States had acquired a standing in the Sino-Soviet dispute with room for maneuver. Even if little had been gained toward a Vietnam settlement, the worldwide onus of obstruction of new international relationships in East Asia had been partially overcome. American losses in credibility and prestige were not as great as expected because the weakness of U.S. policy toward China had long been apparent to all.

After five years the Chinese retained all the advantages won at Shanghai. But they felt cheated over Taiwan. American troops on Taiwan reached new high levels after Shanghai, though they dropped to two thousand by 1976. American F-4 squadrons were introduced onto the island; these were later withdrawn but their appearance as stand-ins for Nationalist planes loaned to Vietnam reminded the Chinese of much. A contract for the manufacture of F-5s was signed with Taiwan. American economic interests on the island grew and in the United States academic observers began to speculate on Taiwan's future as a large Hong Kong, a possible development welcomed by some as an ingenious solution, deplored by others as a throwback to treaty port days and hence fatal to a sound Sino-American relationship. The Nationalists were allowed by the State Department to open new consulates in the United States, bureaucratic error or bureaucratic sabotage depending on which of Mr. Kissinger's spokesmen was doing the whispering. The United States government appointed a new ambassador at Taipei known for his hawkish views on East Asia and China.

The Washington-Taipei mutual security treaty remained unchanged.

Other failures in working out the communiqué's provisions were acceptable to the Chinese. After an initial spurt, trade languished as it had historically because of lack of suitable Chinese exports. American insensitivity in accepting Vladivostok (territory China claims) as the site for Soviet-American SALT talks was dismissed as just another example of the barbarians' ignorance of history, and the Chinese were not concerned about SALT, anyway. American technology seemed harder to come by than had been foreseen, although the Chinese discovered that American arms sales were a possibility. The United States took exception to Chinese efforts to exploit the exchange agreements for other Chinese interests.

Such, then, were the provisions and the initial results of the Nixon visit to Peking and the Shanghai communiqué. Did they in their modest way constitute anything so consequential as a new era? In his last hours in China Nixon remarked to an audience in Shanghai: "This was the week that changed the world." It was scarcely that. Upon Nixon's return to Washington, the Vice President, Spiro Agnew, proclaimed: "Because of your visit, the Chinese and the American people stand further removed from the kind of confrontation that the world has feared for many decades. And we, the American people, are tremendously grateful for that effort on your part." That statement also seemed somewhat inappropriate, another example of the surrealistic ambience of the visit, and by extension, of the entire so-called new era.

Those who thought in that dawn " 'twas bliss to be alive" had little concrete basis for their rapture. The American disengagement from overcommitment to Southeast Asia had been outlined clearly at Guam in the summer of 1969—in the Nixon Doctrine. This disengagement had been fought by both diplomatic and military bureaucracies. They had been aided in their battles by the emotionally hawkish behavior of Nixon and Kissinger. The prolongation of the Vietnam War, the Cambodian and Laotian invasions, subversions, miscalculations, the Hanoi bombings, the buildup on Taiwan: all seemed to go against the grain of the Nixon Doctrine. But the Chinese, while they reacted to the military buildup on Taiwan, stayed their hand. The Russians stayed theirs. Neither was to risk anything for the sake of helping the Americans extricate themselves. In the end, of course, the American leadership did find its way out of its sticky involvements in Asia's periphery. But by December 1976 the Pentagon was unable to tell *The New York Times* whether fifteen thousand or twenty thousand Americans had been killed in Vietnam between Nixon's first inauguration and the final moment when peace was actually at hand. Then, in the final defeat of South Vietnam, the last remaining American military structure on the mainland of Southeast Asia collapsed in Thailand. Nixon's China policy, admirable in intention and successful in part, seemed curiously irrelevant in these ironic successes of the doctrine that bears Nixon's name, though perhaps not his blessing.

As the dawning era clouded over, the Chinese made one impressive gamble. They invited the deposed Nixon—no longer Mr. President, only Mr. Nixon—back for a visit early in 1976. His successor, Gerald R. Ford, surely prayed that it would be merely a sentimental journey. Coming after the death of Chiang Kai-shek and before the American elections of that bicentennial year (and before Peking's own not-to-be-delayed succession crisis), the visit seemed an ideal means to reinvoke the spirit of Shanghai, and if possible the provisions of the communiqué in which the United States had nearly conceded to the mainland view of the Taiwan question. For the United States actually to cooperate in a "Chinese themselves" resolution of the Taiwan problem, right-wing Republican opposition would have to be muted. Probably the Chinese believed that Nixon could help with that. The American people did not see or hear Nixon's report on his visit. That summary remained among Presidents, so that the American people had to remain content with implied assurances that the visit had been innocuous.

In the months before the death of Mao, American confusion over what had been wrought at Shanghai seemed epidemic. American academics urged immediate normalization of relations with Peking so that the anti-American element in Peking could not undo these ties after Mao's death. The American right, having scored a success in forcing President Ford to drop the word détente from his vocabulary, was not about to allow any new step toward Peking. The Chinese fished in these waters by inviting former Defense Secretary James Schlesinger to visit China. It was significant that Schlesinger had serious political and philosophical (to say nothing of personal) differences with Kissinger. The latter denied that he had held up Schlesinger's invitation, but the denial convinced few newsmen, who had grown accustomed to the Pharisee-like quality of Kissinger's answers. The Secretary of State gently ticked off the Chinese in his General Assembly speech of September 30, 1976, observing that the U.S.-Chinese relationship could not be expected to prosper until the Chinese showed some "sensitivity to our views and concerns."

The Chinese invitation to Schlesinger seemed clearly a bid for U.S. military equipment; the same end seemed the basis for a similar invitation to *The New York Times'* Pentagon-oriented columnist, Drew Middleton; academic writers also took up the arms sale line. When the Secretary of State was asked about this, he denied there had been any talk of arms sales with the Chinese. But then he added: "We believe that the territorial integrity and sovereignty of China is [sic] very important to the world equilibrium, and we would consider it a grave matter if this were to be threatened by an outside power." [23] Newsmen, whose Richter scale of diplomatic language had been badly distorted by the shocks of the Nixon diplomatic style, did not pick up "grave matter." Within a week, and for some time thereafter, State Department officials were inviting attention to the passage (clearly aimed at the Soviet Union), although these same officials had no comment on whether there was a U.S. commitment implied in such language.

Late in 1976 Mao Tse-tung died, and matters by no means

clarified in American minds. For one thing, the succession struggle in China was little involved over foreign affairs. For another, Americans were at a loss for information. With the last Chinese leader of their acquaintance passed from the scene, American observers knew frighteningly little about China's headmen. Hua Kuo-feng at length became the new premier; not until six weeks after his accession did the American office in Peking discover that he was married.

Thus the appurtenances of the new era in Sino-American relations—the visits, the communiqué with its ambiguities and lack of results, and the visit reprised—comprised an unreliable mixture of illusion and substance. It was difficult indeed to discern which was which, and in what proportion the real and the surreal had been combined. As a result, it would have taken enormous confidence to assert that the public had seen the last gloss on the Shanghai communiqué. Equal confidence would have been necessary to say anything about the future of Sino-American relations after the passing of Mao. Intimations of Sino-Soviet rapprochement seemed contrived. American confidence of the advantages of its present maneuvering room in consequence of its new relationship with the PRC likewise seemed founded on shallow analysis and an overestimation of China's real power. A prudent view would perhaps have consisted of relaxed skepticism about Chinese friendship for the United States, modesty about the American place in the Chinese scheme of things, and intense concern over how the working out of the Taiwan issue would affect the United States.

Ambiguity, then, remained the hallmark of Sino-American relations in the aftermath of the Nixon visit and the Shanghai communiqué. The irony was that the events and documents of February 1972 had opened a new phase of relations without eradicating or even altering significantly the problems, and so the structure, of the preceding era. The question of the late 1970s thus seemed to be how long China and the United States would be able to tolerate the strain of conducting relations in two modes concurrently.

It may seem that such ambiguity and strain should not be

remarkable. Relations between countries are always a mixture of positive and negative, of goodwill and irritation, conflicts of interest and convergences of interest. But one anomaly of Chinese attitudes in foreign affairs seemed likely to continue to place unusual stress on China's relations with the United States, namely, the Sinocentrism mentioned previously. As a world power, the United States was accustomed to being treated not always with friendship, but with a certain regard; China was still capable of large indifference to the United States. Further, the United States was prepared to treat China like a world power; but China refused to respond as one. That aberrance would in all likelihood continue to strain the understanding, the patience, and the policy of the United States. It would also, and this was of highest consequence, continue to deny to the United States the full measure of benefit in Soviet-American relations that it expected to derive from post-Shanghai relations with China.

Notes

[1] Peter Fleming, *One's Company* (London, 1934, 1950), p. 173.

[2] John Gittings, *The World and China, 1922–1972* (New York, 1974), p. 8.

[3] Warren I. Cohen, *America's Response to China* (New York, 1971), p. 101.

[4] Benjamin I. Schwartz, *Chinese Communism and the Rise of Mao* (Cambridge, 1957), pp. 203, 204.

[5] Kenneth E. Shewmaker, *Americans and Chinese Communists, 1927–1945: A Persuading Encounter* (Ithaca, N.Y., 1971).

[6] *United States Relations with China, with Special Reference to the Period 1944–1949* (Washington, D.C., 1949), hereafter the White Paper. See E. J. Kahn, Jr., *The China Hands* (New York, 1975), and O. Edmund Clubb, *The Witness and I* (New York, 1974).

[7] Ross Y. Koen, *The China Lobby in American Politics* (New York, 1960), p. vii. Koen's book was withheld from distribution for years, save for a few library copies, because of pressure from the Chinese Nationalist and United States governments.

[8] Warren I. Cohen, "The Development of Chinese Communist Policy Toward the United States, 1922–1933," *Orbis*, XI, No. 1 (Spring 1967), p. 221.

[9] Quoted in Cohen, *America's Response to China, op. cit.*, p. 182.

[10] See Davies' analysis in the White Paper, p. 573.

[11] The White Paper, pp. 99, 100.

[12] Quoted in John Paton Davies, Jr., *Dragon by the Tail: American, British, Japanese, and Russian Encounters with China and One Another* (New York, 1972), p. 381.

[13] The White Paper, p. 894.

[14] *Foreign Relations of the United States: 1948*, VIII, p. 317.

[15] A Royal Navy frigate went to the aid of one burning American ship, but the skipper prefaced his help with a call on the loud-hailer that His Majesty's Navy was not interfering in any private war, merely lending humanitarian assistance.

[16] The White Paper, p. xvii. A former State Department officer has written that "Dean Acheson demonstrated the typical parochialism of the older Establishment in his inattention to and maladroit handling of relations with Latin America and East Asia. . . ." Charles Maechling, Jr., "Foreign Policy Makers: The Weakest Link?" *The Virginia Quarterly Review*, 52, No. 1 (Winter 1976), p. 16.

[17] Jacques Guillermaz, *A History of the Chinese Communist Party, 1921–1949* (New York, 1972), p. 434, originally published in Paris in 1968 as *Histoire du parti communiste chinois, 1921–1949*.

[18] An American Sinologue recently told his Chinese escort that the school books he saw contained much anti-American material of the Korean War variety. The escort defended the material as correct, but added: "When we have the money, we'll get new ones." The reverse could probably be duplicated in many American school districts, but in a China just becoming literate the effect is different.

[19] *The Pattern of Sino-American Crises; Political-Military Interactions in the 1950s* (New York, 1975).

[20] *The Pentagon Papers* (Bantam edition, New York, 1971), p. 29.

[21] Simon Leys (pseudonym for Pierre Rymans, a Belgian art historian) has called attention to this point in his recent book, *Chinese Shadows* (New York, 1977). Unfortunately, this interesting volume, by a man who has spent considerable time in Peking in close discussion with higher echelon Chinese officials, appeared too late for the present authors to use.

[22] The Department of State *Bulletin*, LXVI, No. 1708 (March 20, 1972), contains the communiqué (pp. 435–438) and other documentation on the visit.

[23] The Department of State *Bulletin*, LXVV, No. 1950 (November 8, 1976), p. 579.

Readings and Sources

Bulletin of the Department of State (weekly). This publication contains documentation for contemporary American foreign affairs, and is especially valuable for the years that *Foreign Relations of the United States* has not yet covered.

Clubb, O. Edmund, *The Witness and I* (New York, 1974). A former foreign service officer, Clubb presents a sobering account of his experiences with loyalty and security investigators in the McCarthy era.

Cohen, Warren I., *America's Response to China* (New York, 1971). This brief book contains both information and questions of interest to students of Asian-American relations.

Davies, John Paton, Jr., *Dragon by the Tail: American, British, Japanese, and Russian Encounters with China and One Another* (New York, 1972). Elegant writing and good sense mark this fine memoir.

Foreign Relations of the United States (Washington, D.C., various). These volumes contain the basic outline documentation of American foreign policy.

Gittings, John, *The World and China, 1922–1972* (New York, 1974). The effect of this volume's fine scholarship is weakened by overstrained interpretation.

Guillermaz, Jacques, *A History of the Chinese Communist Party, 1921–1949* (New York, 1972). This book is earning high and justified praise for sound scholarship and helpful presentation of material.

―――, *The Chinese Communist Party in Power, 1949–1976* (Boulder, Colo., 1977). Here Guillermaz continues his excellent, monumental study.

Kahn, E. J., Jr., *The China Hands: America's Foreign Service Officers and What Befell Them* (New York, 1975). This sympathetic summary underlines in human terms the American paranoia about China.

Kalicki, J. H., *The Pattern of Sino-American Crises: Political-Military Interactions in the 1950s* (New York, 1975). This book is a solid and useful analysis of an unhappy era in Chinese-American affairs.

Koen, Ross Y., *The China Lobby in American Politics* (New York, 1960). This book was sensational; it is still disconcerting in its elaboration of the connections and maneuvers of the China Lobby in the United States.

The Pentagon Papers (Bantam edition, New York, 1972). Although it is less extensive than the official publication of papers mentioned in the bibliography to chapter five, this version of the Pentagon Papers is more widely available and convenient to use for a general readership. The documents, of course, are both fascinating and essential.

Schwartz, Benjamin I., *Chinese Communism and the Rise of Mao* (Cambridge, Mass., 1957). Long a classic, this volume remains of value.

Shewmaker, Kenneth E., *Americans and Chinese Communists, 1927–1945: A Persuading Encounter* (Ithaca, N.Y., 1971). This fine study must be used on its topic.

Thomson, James C., Jr., *While China Faced West: American Reformers in Nationalist China, 1928–1937* (Cambridge, Mass., 1969). Based on Western sources, this book is an interesting companion to Shewmaker's.

United States Relations with China, with Special Reference to the Period 1944–1949 (Washington, D.C., 1949). The famous White Paper is a durable source of information and documentation on American China policy in the period named.

Notes on Contributors

William J. Brinker, with a Ph.D. in history from Indiana University, teaches in the department of history at Tennessee Technological University, Cookeville, Tennessee.

Frederick B. Hoyt wrote his dissertation at the University of Wisconsin on the subject of Americans in China from 1925 to 1937. The author of several articles, he teaches in the department of history at Illinois State University.

Eugene P. Trani, assistant to the Vice President for Academic Affairs at the University of Nebraska, formerly taught history at Southern Illinois University. He is the author of *The Treaty of Portsmouth: An Adventure in American Diplomacy* (Lexington, Mass., 1969) and co-author of *The Presidency of Warren G. Harding* (Lawrence, Kans., 1977). He has also written many articles on American foreign affairs of the 1920s.

Raymond A. Esthus, professor of history at Newcomb College, Tulane University, has established himself as an authority on American foreign affairs of the early twentieth century. Among his books is *Theodore Roosevelt and the Rise of Japan* (Seattle, Wash., 1966). He has also written numerous articles for scholarly publications.

David F. Trask, Director of the Historical Office of the United States Department of State, until recently was professor of history at the State University of New York at Stony Brook. The author of many monographs and articles, he is especially known for *The United States in the Supreme War Council: American War Aims and Inter-Allied Strategy, 1917–1918* (Middletown, Conn., 1961) and for *Captains and Cabinets: Anglo-American Naval Relations, 1917–1918* (Columbia, Mo., 1972).

Thomas H. Etzold, professor of strategy at the United States Naval War College, is the author of *The Conduct of American Foreign Relations: The Other Side of Diplomacy* (New York, 1977); editor, with John Lewis Gaddis, of *Containment: Documents on American Policy and Strategy, 1945–1950* (New York, 1977); and author of many articles on American foreign and military affairs. He also edited, with F. Gilbert Chan, *China in the 1920s: Nationalism and Revolution* (New York, 1976).

Jerome K. Holloway, Jr., is recently retired from the Foreign Service, in which he served for some twenty-eight years, much of that time in the Far East. He has written a number of articles for professional magazines and won honorable mention in the annual prize competition of the United States Naval Institute for 1973. He joined the faculty of strategy at the United States Naval War College in 1976.

Index

165

U.S.S.L.

DATE DUE